Madhur Jaffrey's
Quick and Easy
Indian Cookery

Madhur Jaffrey's
Quick and Easy
Indian Cookery

TED SMART

First published in 2001

This edition published for The Book People Ltd, Hall Wood Avenue,
Haydock, St Helens WA11 9UL

1 3 5 7 9 10 8 6 4 2

Text © 2001 Madhur Jaffrey
Photography © 2001 Craig Robertson

First published in the United Kingdom in 2001 by Ebury Press,
Random House, 20 Vauxhall Bridge Road, London SW1V 2SA

www.randomhouse.co.uk

Random House Australia (Pty) Limited
20 Alfred Street, Milsons Point, Sydney,
New South Wales 2061, Australia

Random House New Zealand Limited
18 Poland Road, Glenfield,
Auckland 10, New Zealand

Random House South Africa (Pty) Limited
Endulini, 5A Jubilee Road
Parktown 2193, South Africa

The Random House Group Limited Reg. No. 954009

A CIP catalogue record for this book is available from the British Library.

ISBN 0 09 188112 9

Design: Christine Wood
Photography: Craig Robertson
Stylist: Helen Trent
Food stylist: Julie Beresford

Printed and bound in Singapore by Tien Wah Press

contents

introduction

'Are there any Indian recipes that are quick and easy?' I am asked this question often. You have only to come to my home for dinner to know that there are – hundreds of them. You have to come during a weekday when I am also writing for 12–14 hours (or acting or gardening) and have barely time to sneeze. My husband and I eat well, even on those days.

Let's face it. There is no way to get instant marvellous food. If that is what you want, it can only be had at a restaurant (and not always there) or in somebody else's home. But this book may help you come close. Some effort has to be expended in having a well-stocked larder and in some daily shopping. After that, there will be some chopping and stirring, but this can all happen, on the whole, within 30 minutes.

The secret lies in not being too ambitious. Have just a satisfying soup and salad for lunch, perhaps a vindaloo, plain rice and quickly stir-fried vegetable for dinner. For breakfast on Sundays there are wonderfully spicy omelettes to be had, and for tea, how about onion fritters?

Do not be afraid to combine Indian main courses with Western side dishes: spicy fried fish with boiled potatoes and a green salad, an egg curry with toast. Indian breads are somewhat complicated to make, so get them from your local Indian restaurant or take-away or a supermarket to go with your home-made kebab or curry.

Also, do not be afraid of the long list of spices in some recipes. I have stayed away from dishes that require a lot of stirring or have too many steps. But stay away from too many spices? That would be like asking an Indian not to be Indian! If you can put one spice into a pan, you can just as easily put in ten or even fifteen of them. They will all cook quickly and easily. I can assure you of that.

With a few exceptions, the recipes in this book can be prepared and cooked within 30 minutes. Although this calls for a pressure cooker in a small number of cases, its use is not essential. The cooking time will be longer without one, but the ingredients are quickly and easily prepared and the actual cooking methods are simple and trouble-free. Spices and seasonings are available from Indian grocers and many supermarkets. Ingredients are also available by mail order (see page 140).

Follow one set of measurements only. Do not mix imperial and metric. Herbs, fruit juices, etc. are fresh unless otherwise stated. Tablespoon measurements are level unless otherwise stated.

notes on
recipes
notes on
recipes
notes on
recipes
notes on
recipes
notes on
recipes

While the premise of this book does not suggest that you sit down to three-course meals, my own feeling is, why not have the choice? The soups may be had by themselves for lunch, the chicken and prawn dishes may be served with drinks and the onion fritters and sandwiches may be eaten with tea. If you feel like putting together several quick-cooking dishes to make up a grander dinner, these recipes will help you out with the first course.

CONTENTS

soups, appetizers and snacks

ONION FRITTERS
Pyazki bhajia

Serves 6

INGREDIENTS

1 large egg

1 tablespoon lemon juice

100g (3½ oz) chickpea flour (also called gram flour or besan)

¾ teaspoon salt

½ teaspoon chilli powder

½ teaspoon store-bought garam masala

½ teaspoon cumin seeds

1 teaspoon ground cumin

¼ teaspoon ground turmeric

1 fresh, hot green chilli, finely chopped

2 tablespoons chopped green coriander

Vegetable oil for deep-frying

200 g (7 oz) onions, peeled and chopped into medium-sized dice

Even though these are served as a first course in many restaurants – and there is no reason why they should not be – in India they are generally served as a snack with tea. They may also be served with drinks. This particular recipe, in which an egg is used in the batter, comes from my friend, Badi Uzzaman, who played the part of my husband in the television series Firm Friends.

Fresh Green Chutney (p. 120) should be served on the side.

Break the egg into a bowl and beat well. Add 4 tablespoons water and the lemon juice. Mix. Add all the chickpea flour and mix well with a whisk. Put in the salt, chilli powder, garam masala, cumin seeds, ground cumin, turmeric, green chilli and green coriander. Mix well and set aside for at least 10 minutes or longer. Mix again with a whisk. The batter should be of a droppable consistency.

Put the oil for deep-frying in a wok or deep-fryer and set over medium heat. You should have at least 7.5 cm (3 inches) oil in the centre of the wok. When hot, put the onions into the batter and mix. (This should always be done just before frying). Remove heaping teaspoons of the batter and drop it into the hot oil. Use up all the batter this way. Stir and fry the fritters for 7–8 minutes or until they are a golden-red. Remove the fritters with a slotted spoon and drain on a plate lined with paper towels. Serve hot, as soon as the fritters are made.

SANDWICHES WITH MINT AND CHILLI BUTTER

Pudinay aur mirch ki sandwich

Serves 10

INGREDIENTS

85 g (3 oz) softened, unsalted butter

1 teaspoon lemon juice

10 mint leaves, finely chopped

½–1 fresh, hot green chilli, finely chopped

A generous pinch of salt

Freshly ground black pepper

10 thin slices sandwich bread

3–4 lettuce leaves, washed, dried and cut into fine, long slivers

No proper Indian tea was ever served without proper English sandwiches though our idea of 'proper' often managed to be something slightly spicy.

Combine the butter, lemon juice, mint, green chilli, salt and black pepper. Mix well. Butter each slice of bread generously on one side. Put 2 slices together, buttered sides meeting each other. Cut off the crusts and then cut the sandwiches in halves, diagonally. Spread most of the lettuce in a serving plate. Arrange the sandwiches on top. Spread a few of the lettuce shreds over the sandwiches and serve.

GINGERY CAULIFLOWER SOUP

Gobi ka soup

Serves 4–6

INGREDIENTS

3 tablespoons vegetable oil

175 g (6 oz) onions, peeled and chopped

2.5 cm (1 inch) piece fresh ginger, peeled and cut into fine slivers

4 cloves garlic, peeled and chopped

1 teaspoon ground cumin

2 teaspoons ground coriander

¼ teaspoon ground turmeric

⅛–¼ teaspoon chilli powder

225 g (8 oz) potatoes, peeled and cut into rough 1 cm (½ inch) dice

225 g (8 oz) cauliflower florets

1.2 litres (2 pints) chicken stock

Salt if needed

150 ml (5 fl oz) single cream

This soup may be served as an elegant first course at a grand dinner or as part of a simple lunch accompanied, perhaps, by a sandwich or salad or both. It may be made a day in advance and refrigerated. Re-heat gently.

It is a good idea to have the cumin, coriander, turmeric and chilli powder all measured into a small bowl before you start as they go in together and cook very briefly.

Set the oil over highish heat in a good-sized saucepan. When hot, put in the onions, ginger and garlic. Stir and fry for about 4 minutes or until the onions are somewhat browned. Put in the cumin, coriander, turmeric and chilli powder. Stir once and put in the potatoes, cauliflower and chicken stock. If the stock is unsalted, put in ¾ teaspoon salt. Stir and bring to a boil. Cover, turn the heat to low and simmer gently for 10 minutes or until the potatoes are tender. Taste for salt, adding more if you like.

Put the soup into a blender, in 2 batches or more as required, and blend thoroughly. Strain, pushing down to get all the pulp. Add the cream and mix. The soup may now be re-heated and served.

A LIGHT, COLD YOGHURT SOUP
Safed shorva

Serves 4

INGREDIENTS

600 ml (1 pint) natural yoghurt

900 ml (1½ pints) chicken stock

½ teaspoon peeled fresh ginger, grated to a pulp

8 tablespoons peeled, finely diced cucumber

8 tablespoons skinned, de-seeded, finely diced tomato

⅛ teaspoon chilli powder

2 tablespoons finely chopped fresh mint or green coriander or a mixture of both

Salt to taste

Freshly ground black pepper

A light, delightful cold soup for a warm summer day. And, it needs no cooking! I tend to make mine with low-fat yoghurt but you could just as easily use the creamier variety.

If you are in a real hurry, you could chop up the tomato without skinning it but it is preferable – and it does not take that much longer – to skin and de-seed it first. To do this, just throw it (I use one large tomato) into boiling water for 15 seconds and then skin it. After that, cut it into half, crossways, and gently squeeze out all the seeds. Now dice the shell.

If you are using home-made chicken stock for this recipe, make sure that it comes straight out of the refrigerator. Strain it so that no particles of congealed fat fall into the soup.

Put the yoghurt in a bowl. Beat with a fork until smooth and creamy. Slowly add the stock, mixing it in as you do so. Add all the remaining ingredients and mix. Refrigerate until needed. Stir well before serving.

EASY CHICKEN KEBABS
Murgh tikka

Serves 4

INGREDIENTS

4 boned, skinned chicken breast halves (about 560 g/1¼ lb)

¾ teaspoon salt

2 tablespoons lemon juice

3 tablespoons natural yoghurt

1 tablespoon chickpea flour (also called gram flour or besan)

1 teaspoon peeled, very finely grated fresh ginger

2 cloves garlic, peeled and crushed to a pulp

¼ teaspoon chilli powder

¼ teaspoon ground turmeric

½ teaspoon ground cumin

½ teaspoon home-made garam masala (p. 138)

4 tablespoons melted butter or vegetable oil for basting

You may serve these kebabs with drinks, as a first course or even as a light main dish. The pieces of meat may be skewered before grilling or they may be just spread out on a grilling tray.

Cut each breast half into halves, lengthways, and cut crossways into 2.5 cm (1 inch) pieces. Put in a bowl. Rub with ½ teaspoon of the salt and the lemon juice.

Put the yoghurt into a separate small bowl. Add the chickpea flour and mix well. Now put in the remaining ¼ teaspoon salt, ginger, garlic, chilli powder, turmeric, cumin and garam masala. Mix well. Pour this mixture over the chicken pieces. Mix well and set aside for 15 minutes or longer (you could even leave it overnight).

Pre-heat the grill.

Thread the chicken pieces on to 4 skewers and balance the skewers on the raised edges of a grill rack. You could, as an alternative, spread the chicken pieces out on the grilling tray. Baste with the melted butter or oil. Grill about 10 cm (4 inches) from the source of heat for 5 minutes, basting once during this time. Turn the chicken pieces over, baste again and grill for 2–3 minutes or until the chicken pieces are just cooked through. Serve immediately.

CHICKEN LIVERS WITH FENNEL AND BLACK PEPPER

Murgh ki masedar kaleji

Serves 4–8

Cook these livers lightly so there is just a hint of pink inside them. You may serve them as a first course or on toast as a snack.

INGREDIENTS

¼ teaspoon ground turmeric

1 teaspoon ground cumin

1 teaspoon ground coriander

¼ teaspoon chilli powder

1 tablespoon grainy French mustard

3 tablespoons vegetable oil

¼ teaspoon fennel or anise seeds

10 fresh curry leaves, if available

3 cloves garlic, peeled and finely chopped

450 g (1 lb) chicken livers, trimmed and separated into 2 lobes each

Salt

Freshly ground black pepper

8 tablespoons single cream

3 tablespoons finely chopped green coriander

Put the turmeric, cumin, coriander, chilli powder and mustard into a small bowl along with 2 tablespoons water. Mix together well and set this spice paste aside.

Put the oil in a wok or a frying pan and set over high heat. When hot, put in the fennel seeds, curry leaves and garlic. Stir and fry until the garlic turns golden. Put in the chicken livers. Sprinkle with ½ teaspoon salt and lots of black pepper. Stir and toss for 3–4 minutes or until nicely browned. Remove the livers with a slotted spoon and put in a serving dish or bowl. Put in the spice paste. Stir for 15 seconds or so. Put in the cream and a light sprinkling of salt. Stir for 30–60 seconds or until the cream is slightly reduced. Pour the sauce over the chicken livers, sprinkle the green coriander over the top and serve.

DELICIOUS CHICKEN BITS

Murgh ke mazedar tukray

Serves 6–8

INGREDIENTS

560 g (1¼ lb) boned, skinned chicken breasts (4 breast pieces)

1 teaspoon freshly ground black pepper

¼ teaspoon ground turmeric

¼ teaspoon chilli powder

1 teaspoon ground cumin

1 teaspoon dried thyme

¼ teaspoon garlic powder

1 teaspoon bright red paprika

¼ teaspoon salt

About 3 tablespoons vegetable oil

These wonderful chicken cubes may be served hot, warm or cold. They may be pierced with toothpicks and nibbled upon with drinks, added to salads or eaten at picnics. The last is what I did most recently just before I watched my youngest daughter perform the part of Miranda in a summer production of Shakespeare's Tempest *set in a park. (The chicken bits may also be eaten as a main course with rice or potatoes and a green salad, when this recipe will serve four.)*

You may be surprised by my use of thyme. It tastes somewhat like our ajwain seeds, which are much harder to find. If you can get these, use about ⅓ teaspoon only as they are quite strong in flavour. The spice mixture I have used here is an excellent one to have on hand. It may be mixed in advance in the correct proportions (just the dry seasonings, not the oil) and then used when grilling fish, steaks and chops.

Pre-heat the oven to gas mark 4, 350°F (190°C).

Cut each chicken breast piece into thirds, lengthways, and then crossways into 2–2.5 cm (¾–1 inch) segments. Put in a bowl. Add the black pepper, turmeric, chilli powder, cumin, thyme, garlic powder, paprika, salt and 1 tablespoon of the oil. Mix well and set aside for 10 minutes or longer.

Heat 2 tablespoons oil in a wok or large, non-stick frying pan over very high heat. When very hot, put in the chicken. Stir and fry quickly until the chicken pieces are lightly browned or turn opaque on the outside. Put in a baking dish, cover loosely with lightly oiled waxed paper which should sit inside the dish and directly on the chicken pieces, and bake for about 8–10 minutes or until the chicken pieces are just cooked through. If not eating immediately, remove the chicken pieces from the hot baking dish to prevent them from drying out.

PRAWNS WITH GARLIC AND CHILLIES

Lehsun vali jhinga

Serves 6–8

INGREDIENTS

450 g (1 lb) medium-sized, uncooked, unpeeled prawns, peeled, deveined and washed (p. 134), then patted dry

¼ teaspoon ground turmeric

¼ teaspoon chilli powder

½ teaspoon black or yellow mustard seeds

4 tablespoons vegetable oil

5 cloves garlic, peeled and finely chopped

1 fresh, hot green chilli, finely chopped

½ teaspoon salt

2 teaspoons finely chopped green coriander or parsley

Prawns cook so fast. The only time you will spend here is in peeling and deveining them. I like to do this ahead of time and then keep them, washed and patted dry, in a polythene bag in the refrigerator, just ready to be stir-fried. They are perfect as a cocktail snack with toothpicks stuck in them, and also as a first course. You may serve them as a main dish as well. You will find that this recipe will serve six people as a first course or three to four people as a main one.

Put the prawns in a bowl. Sprinkle the turmeric and chilli powder over them evenly and rub in.

Put the oil in a wok or large frying pan and set over high heat. When very hot, put in the mustard seeds. As soon as they begin to pop – this takes just a few seconds – put in the garlic. Stir until the garlic has turned golden. Put in the green chilli. Stir once or twice. Put in the prawns. Stir and fry them over high heat until they just turn opaque. This will take 2–3 minutes. Sprinkle with salt and toss. Finally, sprinkle with the green coriander, then toss and serve.

Apart from quick kebabs and stir-fries like jhal firezi (p. 34), most Indian meat dishes are stewed. Stewed slowly. So this was, potentially, the hardest chapter for me to put together. I knew I could use a pressure-cooker. Most of my Indian relatives do. But I had always hated pressure-cookers. The one I had hissed threateningly and was impossible to open once it had been shut. I always had to call out to my husband to come and prise the lid away from the pot. Also, its shape was all wrong. I like wide pots that allow me to stir and brown the meat.

Just about the time that I had started working on this book, I heard about the Swiss-made, Kuhn Rikon pressure-cookers and ordered one for myself that had the shape of a deep frying pan. I fell in love with it. (More about it at the back of the book.) It worked magically and what is more, had a stainless steel bottom that seemed to have the qualities of a non-stick one. I was sold.

I have selected dishes for this chapter that do not require time spent browning spice pastes, a task specially invented by some malevolent god to teach Indians patience. Everything tends to get thrown into the pot at once and any browning that is done is done at the end – which is much easier as it almost happens by itself.

CONTENTS

beef, lamb
and pork
beef, lamb
and pork
beef, lamb
and pork
beef, lamb
and pork
beef, lamb
and pork
beef, lamb
and pork

'HAMBURGER' KEBABS
Chappal kebab

Serves 4–5

INGREDIENTS

1 tablespoon chickpea flour (also called gram flour or besan)

675 g (1½ lb) minced beef or lamb put thrice through the mincer (it should be quite fine – the butcher could do this)

6–7 tablespoons coarsely chopped green coriander

2 or more fresh, hot green chillies, cut into fine rounds and chopped

1½ teaspoons cumin seeds

1½ teaspoons coriander seeds

1 teaspoon freshly ground black pepper

1¼ teaspoons salt

½ lightly beaten egg

3–4 tablespoons vegetable oil

Forgive this long preamble. Let me say at the very start that these kebabs are utterly delicious and can be prepared – from start to finish – in as little as 15 minutes. Now let me tell you this story.

One of my very good Indian friends – I always call her a hill woman as she is from the mountainous Himalayan region – was convalescing in bed in New York, recovering from an operation. I had taken some of the season's freshest cherries to cheer her up. She was duly grateful but as we talked and she nibbled on the cherries, I realized that her mind was on something else. Did I know of a restaurant that served chappali kebabs? I did not know, nor had I heard of these kebabs. Well, she suggested, they were a real treat. So could I go with her husband right away, have some kebabs at this restaurant and then bring some back for her as well. She gave us an address.

It turned out to be the address of the wrong restaurant. Her husband and I ate some rather pitiful kebabs and, what is more, he took back four orders to please his bedridden wife.

All this started me off on a quest, the first part of which was to find the right place, which my friend now remembered. The other part was to get the recipe from the owners. The right place was hard enough to find as it was in the very seedy Times Square district of New York, had no sign outside and looked like a video shop – which it also was. But once I had found it and managed to taste the wonderful kebabs, getting the recipe was even harder. The owner just kept saying that these kebabs, which were really like thin, spicy and utterly mouth-watering hamburgers, were made of 'meat and spices' and that they were a speciality of the Pakistani city of Peshawar. So I did the next best thing.

I bought a half a dozen kebabs, took them to the car where my husband waited and then dissected and analysed them as we gobbled them up.

I think I have got it! And here it is.

These kebabs are meant to be very spicy. I have used just two green chillies but you could use one whole chilli per kebab if you are up to it. They may be eaten with rice and vegetables but are best cut in halves and rolled up in a flat bread – such as a store-bought pitta or chapati or naan – along with a little salad and either some Fresh Green Chutney (p. 120) or Fresh Red Chutney with Almonds (p. 121). You could also eat them like a hamburger, in a hamburger bun. Again, a little salad and fresh chutney should be sandwiched in as well.

Small versions of these kebabs may be served with drinks.

Put the chickpea flour in a small cast-iron frying pan and stir around over medium heat until it has turned a light brown colour. Put it into a bowl. Add all the other ingredients except the oil and mix well. Form ten 5 cm (2 inch) balls. Flatten the balls to make ten 9 cm (3½ inch) hamburger-like discs. Just before eating, put 2 tablespoons of the oil into a large non-stick frying pan and set over medium-high heat. When hot, put in as many kebabs as the pan will hold in a single layer. Turning them over every 30 seconds or so, cook the kebabs for about 2½ minutes or until they have browned on both sides. Remove to a warm plate. Use the remaining oil to cook a second batch the same way.

LAMB STEWED IN COCONUT MILK
Safed gosht

Serves 4

INGREDIENTS

3 tablespoons vegetable oil

12 fresh curry leaves, if available, or 3 bay leaves

5 cm (2 inch) cinnamon stick

6 cardamom pods

8 cloves

15 black peppercorns

85 g (3 oz) onions, peeled and chopped

675 g (1½ lb) boned shoulder of lamb, cut into 4 cm (1½ inch) chunks

450g (1 lb) potatoes, peeled and cut into pieces the same size as the meat

2 medium-sized carrots, peeled and cut into 3 pieces each

¼ teaspoon ground turmeric

1 tablespoon ground coriander

⅛–½ teaspoon chilli powder

1–2 fresh, hot green chillies

1¼ teaspoons salt

One 400 g (14 oz) tin coconut milk, well stirred

This is a meal in itself, a kind of Indian, Lancashire hot-pot that requires only rice – or a good crusty bread, if you like – on the side. I always serve something green as well, such as Stir-Fried Green Cabbage with Fennel Seeds (p. 80), but a simple green salad would be equally good.

I have used a pressure-cooker for speed. The cooking time in a saucepan would be about 70 minutes and you would need to add 150 ml (5 fl oz) water before starting to cook.

This stew may be made up to a day ahead and re-heated.

Put the oil in a pressure-cooker and set over medium-high heat. When hot, put in the curry leaves, cinnamon, cardamom, cloves and peppercorns. Stir once and put in the onions. Sauté for 1½ minutes or until the onions are soft, and put in the meat, potatoes, carrots, turmeric, coriander, chilli powder, green chillies, salt and 250 ml (8 fl oz) of the well-stirred coconut milk. Cover securely with the lid and, on high heat, bring up to full pressure. Turn the heat to low and cook for 15 minutes. Lower the pressure with the help of cool water and remove the lid. Cook, uncovered, over high heat for 5 minutes, stirring gently as you do this. Add the remaining coconut milk and bring to a simmer. Turn off the heat.

LAMB WITH CARDAMOM
Elaichi gosht

Serves 6

INGREDIENTS

2 tablespoons cardamom pods (the green kind sold by Indian grocers are best)

3 tablespoons vegetable oil

900 g (2 lb) boned shoulder of lamb, cut into 2.5 cm (1 inch) cubes

2 large tomatoes, chopped

4 tablespoons finely chopped onions (red onions or shallots are ideal but any onions will do)

1½ teaspoons store-bought garam masala

1 tablespoon tomato purée

1½ teaspoons salt or to taste

Lots of freshly ground black pepper

Many versions of this dish exist among the Sindhi community of India. This recipe comes from Draupadiji, a veritable treasure house of Sindhi specialities.

Here the green cardamom pods are ground whole, skin and all. This may be done in a clean coffee grinder or other spice grinder or even in a good-quality blender.

This mild, aromatic dish – it has no red chillies but plenty of black pepper – is very much like a stew: gentle and soothing. It should have quite a bit of sauce. Sindhis often eat it with bread so serving it with a good, crusty Italian or French loaf would be downright 'authentic'. You may serve a salad or a selection of Indian vegetables on the side.

You do not, of course, have to use a pressure-cooker here. If you use an ordinary saucepan, put in 600 ml (1 pint) water and cook for 1 hour or a bit longer.

Put the cardamom pods into the container of a clean coffee grinder or other spice grinder and grind until you have a fine powder.

Put the oil in a pressure-cooker and set over a medium-high heat. When hot, put in the cardamom powder. Stir once and put in all the meat. Stir over high heat for 2 minutes. Put in the tomatoes and onions. Stir for another 3 minutes. Now put in the garam masala, tomato purée, salt and 450 ml (15 fl oz) water. Cover tightly and bring up to pressure. Turn the heat to low and cook for 15 minutes. Reduce the pressure quickly with cool water and uncover. Re-heat the meat over high heat. Grind in a very generous amount of black pepper and cook, stirring gently, for a minute. Check the salt.

SMOTHERED LAMB (OR PORK OR BEEF)
Labdhara gosht

Serves 3–4

INGREDIENTS

450 g (1 lb) boned shoulder of lamb or pork shoulder or stewing beef, cut into 2.5 cm (1 inch) cubes

115 g (4 oz) peeled and finely chopped onions

2.5 cm (1 inch) piece fresh ginger, peeled and finely chopped

140 g (5 oz) tomatoes, skinned and finely chopped

About ½ teacup finely chopped green coriander

1–2 fresh, hot green chillies, cut into fine rings

¼ teaspoon ground turmeric

2 teaspoons store-bought garam masala

1 teaspoon ground cumin

4 tablespoons natural yoghurt

1 tablespoon tomato purée

¾ teaspoon salt or to taste

3 tablespoons vegetable oil

4 cloves garlic, peeled and finely chopped

Freshly ground black pepper

There may be a fair number of ingredients in this dish but they all go into the pan at almost the same time so the preparation is quite painless. The taste, however, is scrumptious.

If you do not wish to use a pressure-cooker, this dish may just as easily be cooked in a regular saucepan. It will take anywhere from 1 to 1½ hours (the longer time for beef) and you will need to add about 300 ml (5 fl oz) water just before you begin the simmering. (See photograph overleaf.)

Put all the ingredients except the oil, garlic and black pepper into a bowl and mix well.

Put the oil in a pressure-cooker and set over medium-high heat. When hot, put in the garlic. Stir until the garlic pieces turn medium-brown. Now put in the seasoned meat and stir once or twice. Turn the heat to medium. Cover the pressure-cooker tightly and bring up to pressure slowly. Cook lamb and pork for 15 minutes and beef for 20 minutes at full pressure. Reduce the pressure quickly with the help of cool water. Uncover. Cook, uncovered, over high heat until the sauce is thick, stirring gently as you do so. Sprinkle in lots of black pepper and stir again.

THE MOST DELICIOUS MEAT CUBES

Boti gosht

Serves 3–4

INGREDIENTS

3 tablespoons vegetable oil

4 cm (1½ inch) piece fresh ginger, peeled and very finely chopped

4 cloves garlic, peeled and very finely chopped

15 fresh or dried curry leaves, if available

450 g (1 lb) boned shoulder of lamb or pork shoulder, cut into 2.5 cm (1 inch) cubes

2 teaspoons store-bought garam masala

1 teaspoon ground cumin

¼ teaspoon ground turmeric

¼ teaspoon chilli powder

1 fresh, hot green chilli, finely sliced

½ teaspoon salt or to taste

Freshly ground black pepper

1½–2 teaspoons lemon juice

This is, quite simply, an exquisite dish. It has no sauce. The meat cubes are almost like kebabs, except that they are cooked in a saucepan. I have used a pressure-cooker to speed things up, but you could use an ordinary saucepan, add perhaps 175 ml (6 fl oz) water and cook gently for about 50 minutes before uncovering and boiling down the liquid.

In India, this is made with goat meat. In the West, I tend to make it with boned pork shoulder cut into kebab-like cubes. Boned shoulder of lamb would work as well.

You could serve it as a part of an Indian meal with Indian breads or rice or with Indian Mashed Potatoes (p. 96) and Simply Grilled Tomatoes (p. 93), or, for an even easier meal, with plain boiled potatoes and a green salad.

Put the oil in a pressure-cooker and set over medium-high heat. When hot, put in the ginger, garlic and curry leaves. Stir. When the garlic starts to brown, put in the meat. Stir once or twice and turn the heat to medium-low. Now put in the garam masala, cumin, turmeric, chilli powder, green chilli and salt. Stir to mix. Add 2 tablespoons water and cover tightly. Turn the heat to high and bring up to pressure. Lower the heat and cook under pressure for 15 minutes. Remove from the heat and reduce the pressure quickly with the help of cool water. Remove the cover. Cook, uncovered, over high heat until all the liquid has gone and the meat has browned a bit. Stir as you do this. Add lots of freshly ground black pepper and the lemon juice. Stir to mix.

PORK OR LAMB 'VINDALOO'

Vindaloo

Serves 3–4

INGREDIENTS

1½ tablespoons grainy French mustard (see right)

1½ teaspoons ground cumin

¾ teaspoon ground turmeric

½–1 teaspoon chilli powder

1 teaspoon salt

1 teaspoon red wine vinegar

3 tablespoons vegetable oil

115 g (4 oz) onions, peeled and cut into fine half-rings

6 large cloves garlic, peeled and crushed to a pulp

560 g (1¼ lb) boned hand of pork or shoulder of lamb, cut into 2.5 cm (1 inch) cubes

150 ml (5 fl oz) tinned coconut milk, well stirred

The essential ingredients for this Portuguese-inspired Indian dish are wine vinegar and garlic. Additions of mustard seeds, cumin, turmeric and chillies make it specifically colonial Goan.

Most recipes for Vindaloo involve grinding mustard seeds in vinegar. To save this step, I have used grainy French Pommery mustard (Moutarde de Meaux) which already contains vinegar. It works beautifully.

This dish may be made in the pressure-cooker (20 minutes simmering time) or in a frying pan (1 hour or so of simmering). Either way, once the simmering starts the cook can read a book, sleep or have a drink! It is painless cooking.

Vindaloos are hot. Goans would use 4 teaspoons of chilli powder here. Under my husband's 'spare-me' gaze, I have used half a teaspoon to make a mild dish. It is up to you.

Combine the mustard, cumin, turmeric, chilli powder, salt and vinegar in a cup. Mix well.

Put the oil in a large, non-stick frying pan and set over medium-high heat. When hot, put in the onions. Stir and fry until they are medium-brown. Put in the garlic. Stir and fry for 30 seconds. Put in the paste from the cup. Stir and fry for a minute. Put in the meat. Stir and fry for about 3 minutes. Now add in the coconut milk and 150 ml (5 fl oz) water if you are going to cook in a pressure-cooker and 250 ml (8 fl oz) water if you are going to continue to cook in the frying pan. (Transfer to a pressure-cooker at this stage if that is your intention.) Cover and either bring up to pressure, or to a boil if you are using the frying pan. Lower the heat to a simmer and cook for 20 minutes in a pressure-cooker and 60–70 minutes in the frying pan.

BEEF OR LAMB WITH ONION AND GREEN PEPPER

Jhal firezi

Serves 3–4

INGREDIENTS

340 g (12 oz) cooked, boneless roast beef or roast lamb

½ teaspoon freshly ground black pepper

¼–½ teaspoon chilli powder

1 teaspoon ground cumin

1 teaspoon ground coriander

¼ teaspoon ground turmeric

1 teaspoon red wine vinegar

Salt

3 tablespoons vegetable oil

½ teaspoon cumin seeds

½ teaspoon black or yellow mustard seeds

10 fenugreek seeds (optional)

115 g (4 oz) green pepper, de-seeded and cut, lengthways, into 3 mm (⅛ inch) slivers

140 g (5 oz) onions, peeled and cut into fine half-rings

1 teaspoon Worcestershire sauce

An Anglo-Indian speciality, this calls for leftovers of cooked roast beef or roast lamb. Sunday's roast was invariably turned into a delicious jhal firezi *on Mondays by many a family in cities like Calcutta.*

One or two sliced green chillies may be added to this dish at the same time as the green pepper if you want it really hot. It is worth noting that the use of Worcestershire sauce in cooking is fairly typical of Anglo-Indian households.

You may serve this dish with rice, potatoes or breads. The meat is also excellent stuffed into pitta breads together with some shredded lettuce and sliced tomato.

Cut the cooked meat into 5 mm (¼ inch) slices. Now stack a few slices together at a time and cut into 5 mm (¼ inch) slivers. This does not have to be done too evenly.

Combine the black pepper, chilli powder, ground cumin, ground coriander, turmeric, vinegar, ½ teaspoon salt and 2 tablespoons water in a small cup. Mix and set aside.

Put the oil in a large frying pan over medium-high heat. When hot, put in the cumin, mustard and fenugreek seeds. As soon as the mustard seeds begin to pop, put in the green pepper and onion. Stir and fry until the onion has browned quite a bit and the mass of vegetables has reduced. Sprinkle about ⅛ teaspoon salt over the top and stir.

Add the meat and the spice mixture from the cup. Stir rapidly on the same medium-high heat for a minute or so until the meat has heated through. Add the Worcestershire sauce and stir to mix.

BEEF OR LAMB WITH SPINACH
Saag gosht

Serves 4

INGREDIENTS

285 g (10 oz) packet frozen, chopped spinach

285 g (10 oz) onions, peeled and coarsely chopped

5 cm (2 inch) piece fresh ginger, peeled and coarsely chopped

6–8 cloves garlic, peeled

6 tablespoons vegetable oil

3 bay leaves

10 cardamom pods

8 cloves

Two 5 cm (2 inch) cinnamon sticks

600 g (1½ lb) stewing beef or boned shoulder of lamb, cut into 4 cm (1½ inch) pieces

1⅓ teaspoons salt

1 tablespoon ground coriander

1 teaspoon ground cumin

¼–1 teaspoon chilli powder

½ teaspoon home-made (p. 138) or store-bought garam masala

This is the classic dish, prepared in almost every North Indian home and loved by all. To make it quickly, a pressure-cooker is essential. If you use a regular saucepan it will take about 1 hour for lamb to cook and 1½ hours for beef. You will need to increase the amount of water to 600 ml (1 pint). It helps to have a food processor to chop the onion, ginger and garlic finely at great speed.

Drop the spinach into boiling water according to the instructions on the packet and boil just until it is defrosted. Drain the spinach and squeeze out most of the water.

Put the onions, ginger and garlic into the container of a food processor and 'pulse', starting and stopping with great rapidity, until finely chopped.

Put the oil in a pressure-cooker and set over high heat. When hot, put in the bay leaves, cardamom pods, cloves and cinnamon sticks. Stir once or twice and put in the finely chopped seasonings from the food processor. Stir and cook over high heat for 5 minutes. Put in the beef or lamb, the spinach, 450 ml (15 fl oz) water, salt, coriander, cumin and chilli powder. Stir. Cover, securing the pressure-cooker lid, and bring up to full pressure. The beef will take 20 minutes, the lamb 15 minutes. Cool off the pressure-cooker quickly with cool water and remove the lid. Put in the garam masala and bring the contents of the pressure-cooker to a boil again. Cook, uncovered, stirring gently over high heat for about 7–10 minutes or until the sauce is reduced and thick. (Leave the oil behind, when serving.)

LAMB WITH ONIONS
Kaliya

Serves 4

INGREDIENTS

3 tablespoons vegetable oil

250 g (9 oz) onions, peeled and cut into fine half-rings

2.5 cm (1 inch) piece fresh ginger, peeled and cut into fine slivers

6 cloves garlic, peeled and finely chopped

675 g (1½ lb) boned shoulder of lamb, cut into 4 cm (1½ inch) chunks

2–6 fresh, hot green chillies, sliced into rounds

2 tinned plum tomatoes, coarsely chopped, and 6 tablespoons of juice from the tin

6 tablespoons natural yoghurt

1 teaspoon ground roasted cumin seeds (p. 137)

1 teaspoon salt

1 teaspoon home-made garam masala (p. 138)

This is a very simple way to prepare a traditional dish – everything goes into the pressure-cooker together and a lot of fuss is avoided! If you wish to use an ordinary saucepan, increase the juice from the tomato tin to 12–15 tablespoons (water may be used too). Cook for about 50–60 minutes before taking off the lid and reducing the liquid.

Put all the ingredients except the garam masala into a pressure-cooker and mix well. Turn the heat to medium and secure the top of the pressure-cooker. Leave on medium heat for 5 minutes and then turn the heat up to high and build up the pressure. When the pressure is fully up, turn the heat to low and cook for 15 minutes. Reduce the pressure quickly with the help of cool water and open the pot. Add the garam masala and cook, uncovered, over high heat for about 10 minutes or until the sauce is thick and greatly reduced. Stir gently as you do this.

MINCED LAMB WITH TOMATOES AND PEAS

Keema matar

Serves 4–6

INGREDIENTS

115 g (4 oz) onions, peeled and coarsely chopped

5 cm (2 inch) piece fresh ginger, peeled and coarsely chopped

5–6 large cloves garlic, peeled and coarsely chopped

4 tablespoons vegetable oil

½ teaspoon chilli powder

1 teaspoon cumin seeds

1 teaspoon coriander seeds

½ teaspoon turmeric powder

200 g (7 oz) tomatoes, chopped

4 tablespoons natural yoghurt

560 g (1¼ lb) minced lamb

1¼ teaspoons salt

2 teaspoons store-bought garam masala

2 tablespoons lemon juice

1 fresh, hot green chilli, chopped

6 tablespoons coarsely chopped green coriander

140 g (5 oz) peas, fresh or frozen

The quickest method of chopping onion, garlic and ginger finely is to put them into a food processor and use the 'pulse' method: rapidly start and stop the machine until you have the result you want. That is what I have done here.

Put the onions, ginger and garlic into the container of a food processor and chop finely.

Put the oil in a wide, non-stick pan and set over medium-high heat. When hot, put in the finely chopped mixture from the food processor. Stir and fry until it is somewhat brown. Put in the chilli powder, cumin seeds, coriander seeds and turmeric. Stir once or twice. Now put in the tomatoes and yoghurt. Stir on high heat until the tomatoes are soft. Put in the meat, salt and garam masala. Stir, breaking up any lumps, for 2 minutes. Put in 250 ml (8 fl oz) water. Stir and bring to a simmer. Cover, turn the heat to low and simmer for 25 minutes. Add the lemon juice, green chilli, green coriander and peas. Stir and bring to a simmer. Cover the pan and cook on low heat for 10 minutes.

When I was growing up, chicken was considered 'special'. It was really party food but the family could have it on, say, a Saturday evening as a special treat. For me, its aura still remains, even though it is now cheap and easily available. This aura is probably connected with how it was cooked. Because it was not an everyday food, it was prepared in a more interesting manner. Here follow some of the recipes from my childhood. All I have done is simplify some of the techniques to lessen your exertion. The tastes remain the same.

CONTENTS

eggs and
poultry
eggs and
poultry
eggs and
poultry
eggs and
poultry
eggs and
poultry

HARD-BOILED EGGS 'MASALA'

Masaledar ublay unday

Serves 2–4

These can be whipped up quickly for lunch or supper. They may be served with rice or even bread (toasted or plain).

INGREDIENTS

½ teaspoon chilli powder

½ teaspoon ground turmeric

1 teaspoon ground cumin

1 teaspoon ground coriander

1 teaspoon lemon juice

¾ teaspoon salt

Freshly ground black pepper

2 tablespoons vegetable oil

½ teaspoon cumin seeds

75 g (2½ oz) onion, peeled and finely chopped

1 cm (½ inch) piece fresh ginger, peeled and finely chopped

250 ml (8 fl oz) tinned chopped tomatoes (or lightly drained, tinned whole tomatoes, finely chopped)

¼ teaspoon sugar

3–4 tablespoons chopped green coriander

4 hard-boiled eggs, peeled and cut into halves lengthways

Combine the chilli powder, turmeric, ground cumin, ground coriander, lemon juice, salt, black pepper and 1 tablespoon water in a small bowl. Mix. Put the oil in a medium-sized, non-stick frying pan and set over highish heat. When hot, put in the cumin seeds. Ten seconds later, put in the onion and ginger. Stir and fry until the onion turns medium-brown. Put in the spice paste. Stir and cook for 15 seconds. Now put in the tomatoes and sugar. Bring to a simmer. Cover and simmer gently for 10 minutes. Put in the green coriander. Stir once or twice. Lay the cut eggs in the sauce and spoon more sauce over them. Cover and simmer gently for 2–3 minutes.

GARLICKY MUSHROOM 'MASALA' OMELETTE
Masala omlate

Serves 2

INGREDIENTS

5 large eggs

Salt

Freshly ground black pepper

4 tablespoons vegetable oil

½ teaspoon black or yellow mustard seeds

1 large clove garlic, peeled and very finely chopped

4 large or 6 medium-sized mushrooms, sliced lengthways

3 spring onions, cut into very fine rounds (the white as well as the green sections)

1 fresh, hot green chilli, cut into very fine rounds

4 heaped tablespoons coarsely chopped green coriander

½ teaspoon peeled, finely grated, fresh ginger

4 tablespoons tinned chopped tomatoes (see above)

This is an ideal dish for a brunch, a light lunch or even a quick light supper. You may serve it with toast and tea, as in Indian hotels, or with crusty French bread, a green salad and perhaps some cool white wine.

The chopped tomatoes are straight out of a tin. You may substitute tinned whole tomatoes that have been lightly drained and very finely chopped or, in season, use double the quantity of very finely chopped fresh tomatoes. You don't need to skin them.

Break the eggs into a bowl. Add a generous ¼ teaspoon salt and some freshly ground black pepper and beat well. Pour into a glass measuring jug. Put 2 tablespoons of the oil in a medium-sized frying pan and set over high heat. When hot, put in the mustard seeds. As soon as they begin to pop – this takes just a few seconds – put in the garlic. Stir once or twice. As soon as the garlic starts to brown, put in the mushrooms and stir until the mushrooms lose their raw look. Now turn the heat to medium and put in the spring onions, green chilli, green coriander and ginger. Stir until the green seasonings have wilted – about a minute. Put in the tomatoes and a little salt and pepper. Stir for about 30 seconds (or until they are no longer watery for fresh tomatoes) and turn off the heat. This is the stuffing.

Put 1 tablespoon of the oil in an 18 cm (7 inch) non-stick or other omelette pan and set over high heat. When hot, pour in half the beaten eggs. Using a wooden spoon or the back of a fork, stir the eggs for the next 3–4 seconds until they look like lumps of soft custard held together in one unbroken layer. Quickly spread half the stuffing along the centre of the omelette and fold it over. Cook for another few seconds and flip the omelette over on to a warm plate. Make the second one the same way.

EGGS WITH FRESH GREEN HERBS

Hare masale ka omlate

Serves 2–4

INGREDIENTS

5 large eggs

Salt

Freshly ground black pepper

2 tablespoons vegetable oil

3 spring onions, cut into fine rounds (the white as well as the green sections)

¼ teaspoon peeled, very finely chopped garlic

3 tablespoons finely chopped green coriander

1–2 fresh, hot green chillies, sliced into fine rounds

½ teaspoon peeled, very finely chopped fresh ginger

A generous pinch of ground turmeric

1½ teaspoons lemon juice

⅓ teaspoon sugar

This may be served at breakfasts and brunches as soon as it comes out of the frying pan (I serve it with toast) and may also be sliced and put into sandwiches to perk up a picnic or an office lunch. It is really a kind of flat egg pancake seasoned with spring onions, green coriander, green chillies, ginger and garlic.

It is a good idea to have everything cut and ready before you start as this dish cooks very quickly.

Break the eggs into a bowl and beat well. Add a generous ¼ teaspoon salt and lots of freshly ground black pepper.

Put the oil in a large, non-stick frying pan and set over medium-high heat. When hot, put in the spring onions. Stir and fry until the onions just start to brown at the edges. Put in the garlic and stir for a few seconds. Now put in the green coriander, chillies, ginger and turmeric. Stir for a few seconds. Add the lemon juice and sugar and stir to mix. Working quickly, spread the herbs around evenly in the pan. Now pour in the beaten eggs and let them spread to the edges of the pan. Cover, turn the heat to medium-low and cook for a few minutes, just until the eggs have set. Cut into wedges and serve immediately.

CHICKEN BREASTS BAKED WITH GREEN CHILLIES AND ONIONS

Oven ki murghi

Serves 2–4

INGREDIENTS

FOR THE SAUCE:

2 tablespoons tomato purée

1 tablespoon fine, Dijon-type French mustard

1 teaspoon ground cumin

1 teaspoon store-bought garam masala

1 tablespoon lemon juice

½ teaspoon salt

⅛–¼ teaspoon chilli powder

250 ml (8 fl oz) single cream

YOU ALSO NEED:

4 boned, skinned chicken breast halves (about 560 g/1¼ lb)

Salt

Freshly ground black pepper

4 tablespoons vegetable oil

5 cm (2 inch) cinnamon stick

6 cardamom pods

6 cloves

140 g (5 oz) onions, peeled and cut into fine half-rings

2.5 cm (1 inch) piece fresh ginger, peeled and cut into fine slices, then into fine strips

1–3 fresh, hot green chillies, cut at a diagonal into fine strips

This gentle dish is elegant enough to be served at grand dinners. It can easily be doubled or tripled as the guest list expands. It is equally perfect at a dinner for two. In fact, my husband and I dine on it frequently when we are by ourselves. The accompaniment of a simple rice and a vegetable or salad suffices for us but if we are entertaining, I might serve Rice with Mushrooms (p. 108) and Cauliflower with Ginger, Garlic and Green Chillies (p. 84) as side dishes.

By the way, this is a wonderful method for cooking chicken breasts. You will notice that they remain quite tender and very juicy.

Pre-heat the oven to gas mark 4, 350°F (180°C).

Put the tomato purée in a bowl. Add 1 tablespoon water and mix. Add all the remaining ingredients for the sauce in the listed order, mixing as you go. Spread out the chicken pieces. Salt and pepper them generously on both sides.

Put 3 tablespoons of the oil in a non-stick frying pan and set over high heat. When hot, put in the cinnamon, cardamom pods and cloves. Ten seconds later, put in the chicken pieces in a single layer and brown them lightly on both sides. Remove with a slotted spoon and place in an ovenproof dish in a single layer. Put the onions, ginger and green chillies into the oil that remains in the frying pan. Stir and fry them until they are light brown in colour. Remove with a slotted spoon and spread evenly over the chicken pieces.

Add the last tablespoon of oil to the frying pan and let it heat. Put in the mustard seeds. As soon as they pop – this just takes seconds – put in the garlic. Stir. As soon as it starts to brown, pour in the sauce. As soon as the sauce heats up and starts bubbling, pour it over and around the chicken

½ teaspoon black or yellow mustard seeds

1 clove garlic, peeled and finely chopped

without displacing the onion mixture. Place the ovenproof dish, uncovered, in the oven and bake for 25 minutes. Serve immediately.

MINCED CHICKEN (OR TURKEY) WITH PEAS
Murghi ka keema

Serves 3–4

INGREDIENTS

3 tablespoons vegetable oil

2.5 cm (1 inch) cinnamon stick

4 cardamom pods

2 bay leaves

115 g (4 oz) onions, peeled and chopped

3 cloves garlic, peeled and finely chopped

2 teaspoons peeled, finely grated fresh ginger

560 g (1¼ lb) minced chicken (or turkey)

180–200 g (6–7 oz) lightly cooked fresh or frozen peas

¼ teaspoon ground turmeric

1 teaspoon store-bought garam masala

¼ teaspoon chilli powder

½–¾ teaspoon salt

2 tablespoons lemon juice

Freshly ground black pepper

Minced chicken – or turkey, for that matter – cooks in minutes. If a guest unexpectedly shows up, this may be the perfect dish to serve. I have used peas here but infinite variations are possible: cooked broad beans, cut up and cooked green beans, even corn kernels, may be added to the mince.

Put the oil in a wide pan and set over medium-high heat. When hot, put in the cinnamon, cardamom and bay leaves. Stir for a few seconds. Put in the onions. Stir and fry until the onion pieces turn brown at the edges. Put in the garlic and stir for a few seconds. Put in the ginger and stir for another few seconds. Now put in the chicken (or turkey). Stir and fry until all the lumps are broken up. Now put in all the remaining ingredients. Stir to mix and cook for another 2–3 minutes, stirring as you do so.

Note: The large spices are not meant to be eaten.

SPICY GRILLED CHICKEN

Masalewala murgh

Serves 4

INGREDIENTS

FOR THE SPICE PASTE:

1 tablespoon coarsely crushed black peppercorns

1 tablespoon paprika (bright red, if possible)

½ teaspoon chilli powder or to taste

1 tablespoon store-bought garam masala

2 teaspoons ground cumin

2 teaspoons oregano

1 clove garlic, peeled and crushed

1¼ teaspoons salt

3 tablespoons vegetable oil

2 tablespoons lemon juice

2 tablespoons natural yoghurt

YOU ALSO NEED:

1.25 kg (2¾ lb) jointed chicken pieces

Sometimes, after a long day at work, the easiest dish to put at the table is grilled chicken. Most Indian versions require a marinading period but if you are rushed, as I am most of the time, follow this recipe and you will come up with delicious results – fast.

You may be a bit surprised by my use of oregano but it tastes a bit like our Indian ajwain and is much easier to find.

This chicken may be served, Western-style, with boiled potatoes and a green vegetable or salad. You may also serve it with rice and an Indian vegetable, such as Green Peas in a Creamy Sauce (p. 92).

Helpful suggestions: The spice paste may be prepared up to a day ahead of time and refrigerated. You can also rub the chicken pieces with the spice paste and leave them for up to 24 hours before grilling.

Pre-heat the grill and arrange the grilling tray at least 13–15 cm (5–6 inches) from the source of heat. If you can control your heat, set it at medium-high. Combine all the ingredients for the spice paste in a bowl and mix well. Rub the paste over the chicken as evenly as possible. Arrange the chicken pieces on the grilling tray in a single layer, with the fleshier parts up and the skin side down. Grill for 10–12 minutes or until browned. You may need to rearrange some of the pieces so that they all brown evenly. Turn the pieces over and cook the second side in the same way.

CHICKEN IN A GREEN CORIANDER, SPINACH AND MUSTARD SAUCE

Hare masale vala murgh

Serves 3–4

INGREDIENTS

4 tablespoons vegetable oil

3 bay leaves

6 cardamom pods

5 cm (2 inch) cinnamon stick

5 cloves

2 dried, hot red chillies

1 kg (2¼ lb) chicken pieces, skinned and cut into serving portions (a pair of breasts into 4–6 pieces each, whole legs into 2–3 pieces each)

4 tablespoons sultanas

6 tablespoons natural yoghurt

Salt

Freshly ground black pepper

⅛–¼ teaspoon chilli powder

5 cm (2 inch) piece fresh ginger, peeled and coarsely chopped

1–2 fresh, hot green chillies, sliced into coarse rings

I was trying to work out a quick version of a chicken dish seasoned with crushed mustard seeds and vinegar when it occurred to me that instead of grinding the mustard seeds and soaking them in vinegar, I could just as easily use the grainy Pommery mustard that was sitting in a crock in my refrigerator. The taste would be almost the same and I would be saving a step! This particular mustard is labelled Moutarde de Meaux. It also says Pommery on the label. Any grainy French mustard will do.

You can serve this superb dish as part of a grand Indian meal or, as I sometimes do, with Indian Mashed Potatoes (p. 96) and Simply Grilled Tomatoes (p. 93). No other vegetable is needed as the sauce is almost entirely made up of spinach with the green coriander providing an extra dimension of flavour. Of course, you could always serve it with rice, plain boiled potatoes or a bread. (See photograph overleaf.)

A generous fistful of green coriander tops (leaves and bits of tender stems)

285 g (10 oz) packet frozen, chopped spinach, boiled until it is just defrosted and then lightly drained

3 tablespoons Pommery mustard (see opposite)

Put the oil in a large, wide, non-stick pan (a large, non-stick frying pan is also quite suitable) and set over medium-high heat. When hot, put in the bay leaves, cardamom pods, cinnamon stick, cloves and red chillies. Stir for a few seconds or until the bay leaves turn a few shades darker. Now put in the chicken pieces and brown well on both sides. Put in the sultanas and stir for a few seconds. Now put in the yoghurt, 1 teaspoon salt, lots of freshly ground black pepper and the chilli powder. Stir and bring to a simmer. Cover well, turn the heat to low and simmer gently for 15 minutes. While the chicken simmers, put the ginger into the container of a blender along with 3 tablespoons water and blend until you have a smooth paste. Add the green chillies and green coriander and continue to blend, pushing down with a rubber spatula when necessary. Now put in the lightly drained spinach. Blend very briefly this time. The spinach should have a coarse texture and should not be a fine purée. Empty this green sauce into a bowl. Add the mustard and ¼ teaspoon salt. Mix.

When the chicken has cooked for 15 minutes, remove the cover and add the green sauce. Stir to mix. Bring to a simmer, cover again and cook for about 10 minutes or until the chicken is tender. Turn the chicken pieces a few times during this period.

Note: The large whole spices are not meant to be eaten.

SILKEN CHICKEN
Reshmi murgh

Serves 2–4

INGREDIENTS

FOR MARINADING THE CHICKEN:

4 boned, skinned chicken breast halves (about 560 g/1¼ lb)

½ teaspoon salt

2 tablespoons lemon juice

4 tablespoons single cream

½ teaspoon home-made garam masala (p. 138)

¼ teaspoon chilli powder

1 clove garlic, peeled and crushed to a pulp

½ teaspoon peeled, finely grated fresh ginger

¼ teaspoon ground roasted cumin seeds (p. 137)

½ teaspoon paprika

FOR SPRINKLING OVER THE CHICKEN:

Salt

Freshly ground black pepper

A little home-made garam masala (p. 138)

A little ground roasted cumin seeds (p. 137)

A little chilli powder

Generous squeezes of lemon juice

1 teaspoon dried mint flakes

The texture of the chicken here is really soft and silken. As this dish takes just 15 minutes to cook and is best eaten fresh out of the oven, I leave it in its marinade until exactly 15 minutes before we sit down to eat. (It can stay in the marinade for several hours, even overnight, if you like). Sprinkle the extra spice just before the chicken goes into the oven.

These chicken breasts may be served Indian-style with rice and vegetables or Western-style with boiled potatoes and either steamed vegetables or a salad. Both would make for light meals. Leftovers, if there are any, can be covered and refrigerated. They are excellent when sliced and put into sandwiches or salads.

Pre-heat the oven to its highest temperature and arrange a shelf in the top third of the oven.

Cut 3 diagonal slits across the top of each piece of breast, being careful not to go all the way through and also careful not to go to the edge. Prick the chicken pieces with the sharp point of a small knife. Lay them in a large, deepish plate in a single layer and rub both sides with the salt and lemon juice. Leave for 5 minutes. Meanwhile, combine the cream, garam masala, chilli powder, garlic, ginger, ground roasted cumin seeds and paprika in a bowl. Stir this mixture well and pour it over the chicken. Rub it into the meat and leave for 10 minutes.

Lift the chicken pieces up – most of the marinade will cling to them – and lay them down in a single layer on a shallow baking tray lined with foil. On top of each, sprinkle a little salt, black pepper, garam masala, ground roasted cumin seeds, chilli powder, lemon juice and dried mint flakes. Put into the top third of the oven and bake for 15 minutes or until the chicken is just white all the way through. Serve immediately, minted side up.

CHICKEN IN A SPICY RED SAUCE

Lal shorve vala murgh

Serves 3–4

INGREDIENTS

1 kg (2¼ lb) jointed chicken pieces (see opposite)

Salt

Freshly ground black pepper

7 good-sized cloves garlic, peeled and coarsely chopped

5 cm (2 inch) piece fresh ginger, peeled and coarsely chopped

4 tablespoons vegetable oil

A generous pinch of ground asafetida (optional)

1 teaspoon cumin seeds

5 cm (2 inch) cinnamon stick

6 cardamom pods

5 cloves

3 dried, hot red chillies

½ teaspoon ground turmeric

⅛–¼ teaspoon chilli powder

300 ml (10 fl oz) tinned, chopped tomatoes (see above)

340 g (12 oz) potatoes, peeled and cut into 4 cm (1½ inch) chunks

This dish of chicken and potatoes in a delicious red tomato sauce spiced up with cumin, cardamom, garlic and ginger may be served with plain rice or with any Indian or Middle Eastern bread. I use tinned chopped tomatoes but you could use whole tinned ones. Just drain them very lightly and then chop them very finely. Double the amount of fresh tomatoes, in season, may be used in the same way. You do not need to skin them.

I tend to use smallish chicken thighs but you can use any chicken part. A pair of breasts should be cut into 4–6 pieces each and whole legs into 2–3 pieces each. I skin all my chicken pieces but if you are in a great rush, you need not bother.

Sprinkle the chicken pieces lightly with salt and black pepper and set aside. Put the garlic and ginger into the container of a blender along with 3 tablespoons water and blend to a paste.

Put the oil in a wide, non-stick pan and set over medium-high heat. When hot, put in the asafetida if you are using it. A few seconds later, put in the cumin seeds. Wait for 10 seconds and put in the cinnamon stick, cardamom pods, cloves and red chillies. Stir for a few seconds until the large spices begin to turn darker. Now put in the spice paste from the blender. Stir and fry it for about 2 minutes. Put in the chicken, turmeric and chilli powder. Stir and fry for another minute. Now put in the chopped tomatoes, potatoes, 300 ml (10 fl oz) water and 1 teaspoon salt. Bring to a boil. Cover, turn the heat to low and simmer gently for 25–30 minutes or until the chicken and potatoes are tender.

Note: This dish may be made a day ahead of time, kept covered in the refrigerator and then re-heated. The large spices are not meant to be eaten.

CHICKEN, RED LENTILS AND GREEN BEANS IN ONE POT

Ek handi ka murgh aur masoor

Serves 4–6

INGREDIENTS

6 tablespoons vegetable oil

3 bay leaves

5 cloves

6 cardamom pods

5 cm (2 inch) cinnamon stick

3 hot, dried red chillies

900 g (2 lb) chicken pieces, skinned and cut into smaller serving portions (a pair of breasts into 4–6 pieces each and whole legs into 2–3 pieces each)

Red lentils (masoor dal) measured to the 350 ml (12 fl oz) level in a measuring jug, picked over, washed and drained

½ teaspoon ground turmeric

Salt

Freshly ground black pepper

1½ teaspoons store-bought garam masala

1½ tablespoons lemon juice

180 g (6 oz) green beans, trimmed and cut into 2.5 cm (1 inch) lengths

A generous pinch of asafetida (optional)

1½ teaspoons cumin seeds

115 g (4 oz) onions, peeled and cut into fine half-rings

Even though this dish takes 45 minutes to make (from start to finish), almost everything you need for the meal, except the rice or bread, is in the one pan – poultry, lentils, green vegetable, even tomatoes. If you leave out the chillies, this is a perfect dish for children.

I have measured the red lentils by volume here but note that you will need 285 g (10 oz) when you buy them.

There are, indeed, quite a lot of ingredients in the recipe. Do not let that put you off. This is an easy dish to prepare and delicious besides.

Put 3 tablespoons of the oil into a wide, non-stick pan and set over high heat. When hot, put in the bay leaves, cloves, cardamom pods, cinnamon stick and red chillies. Stir once or twice until the bay leaf starts to darken. Quickly put in the chicken pieces in a single layer and brown on both sides. Remove and spread out on a plate, leaving the oil and spices behind. Take the pan briefly off the heat and put into it the lentils, turmeric and 1.2 litres (2 pints) water. Put it back on high heat and bring to a simmer. Cover partially and cook gently for 20 minutes.

Meanwhile, sprinkle ½ teaspoon salt, lots of black pepper, ½ teaspoon of the garam masala and the lemon juice on both sides of the chicken pieces. Rub in and set aside. When the lentils have cooked for 20 minutes, put in the chicken and all its accumulated juices, the green beans and 1½ teaspoons salt. Stir and bring to a simmer. Cover, turn the heat to low and cook gently for another 20 minutes, stirring now and then.

Two minutes before this last 20 minutes is over, put the remaining 3 tablespoons oil in a medium-sized frying pan and set over high heat. When hot, put in the asafetida if you are using it and, a second later, the cumin seeds. Ten seconds later, put in the onions. Stir and fry until the onions turn

2 cloves garlic, peeled and finely chopped

1 teaspoon ground cumin

1 teaspoon ground coriander

⅛–¼ teaspoon chilli powder (optional)

12 cherry tomatoes, cut into halves, crossways, or 140 g (5 oz) plain tomatoes, diced

brown at the edges. Put in the garlic. Stir and fry until the onion has turned fairly brown. Add the ground cumin, ground coriander, 1 teaspoon garam masala, and the chilli powder if you want the dish to be hot. Stir once. Now put in the tomatoes, stir for 30 seconds and pour this entire mixture into the pan with the chicken and lentils. Stir to mix.

QUICK CHICKEN KORMA
Murgh korma

Serves 4

INGREDIENTS

4 cm (1½ inch) piece fresh ginger, peeled and coarsely chopped

5–6 cloves garlic, peeled and coarsely chopped

6 tablespoons vegetable oil

3 bay leaves

5 cm (2 inch) cinnamon stick

8 cardamom pods

4 cloves

¼ teaspoon black cumin seeds (or ordinary cumin seeds)

130 g (4½ oz) onions, peeled and finely chopped

1 tablespoon ground coriander

1 tablespoon ground cumin

3 tinned plum tomatoes, chopped

1.5 kg (3 lb) chicken pieces, skinned and cut into serving portions

¼–1 teaspoon chilli powder

¼ teaspoon salt

3 tablespoons single cream

When trying to cook fast, it helps to have all the right tools and utensils at hand. Here, a blender to make the ginger-garlic paste and a frying pan or sauté pan wide enough to hold all the chicken in a single layer will be of great help. This entire dish can be made a day ahead of time and refrigerated. It re-heats well.

Put the ginger, garlic and 3 tablespoons water in the container of an electric blender. Blend until you have a smooth paste.

Put the oil in a wide frying pan or sauté pan and set over high heat. When very hot, put in the bay leaves, cinnamon, cardamom pods, cloves and cumin seeds. Stir once or twice and put in the onions. Stir and fry for about 3 minutes or until the onions turn brownish. Put in the paste from the blender, and the ground coriander and ground cumin and fry for a minute. Put in the chopped tomatoes and fry for another minute. Put in the chicken, chilli powder, salt and 250 ml (8 fl oz) water. Bring to a boil. Cover, turn the heat to medium and cook for 15 minutes, turning the chicken pieces over now and then. Remove the cover, add the cream and cook on high heat for another 7–8 minutes or until the sauce has thickened. Stir gently as you do this.

ROYAL CHICKEN COOKED IN YOGHURT
Shahi murgh

Serves 4

An elegant dish that may be served to the family or at a grand party. Rice is the ideal accompaniment.

INGREDIENTS

250 ml (8 fl oz) natural yoghurt

1 teaspoon salt

Freshly ground black pepper

1 teaspoon ground cumin

1 teaspoon ground coriander

¼ teaspoon chilli powder, or to taste

4 tablespoons finely chopped green coriander

1.5 kg (3½ lb) chicken, cut into serving portions

4 tablespoons vegetable oil

8 cardamom pods

6 cloves

5 cm (2 inch) cinnamon stick

3 bay leaves

2½ tablespoons blanched, slivered almonds

2½ tablespoons sultanas

Put the yoghurt into a bowl. Beat it lightly until it is smooth and creamy. Add ½ teaspoon of the salt, some black pepper, the ground cumin, ground coriander, chilli powder and green coriander. Mix and set aside.

Salt and pepper the chicken pieces on both sides using the remaining ½ teaspoon salt.

Put the oil in a wide, preferably non-stick pan and set over medium-high heat. When hot, put in the cardamom pods, cloves, cinnamon and bay leaves. Stir once and put in some chicken pieces, only as many as the pan will hold easily in a single layer. Brown on both sides and remove to a large bowl. Brown all the chicken pieces this way and remove to the bowl. Put the almonds and sultanas into the same hot oil. Stir quickly. The almonds should turn golden and the sultanas should plump up – which will happen very fast. Now put the chicken and its accumulated juices back into the pan. Add the seasoned yoghurt. Stir to mix and bring to a simmer. Cover, turn the heat to low and simmer gently for 20 minutes, stirring once or twice during this period. Remove the cover, turn the heat up a bit and reduce the sauce until it is thick and just clings to the chicken pieces. Turn the chicken pieces over gently as you do this.

Note: The large, whole spices are not meant to be eaten.

There is nothing quite as good as fresh fish and more and more

seems to be finding its way into our markets these days. For this I

am very thankful. Fresh fish fillets and steaks can be quickly fried or

grilled with lavish sprinkings of mouthwatering spices. But we should

not discount some tinned and frozen fish. You will find here a superb

recipe for tinned tuna, filled with slivers of fresh ginger, green chillies

and green coriander. Squid freezes very well as do prawns when

they are flash-frozen at sea. Both cook in minutes and can be

combined with green sauces, coconut sauces or spicy tomato-based

sauces, whatever your fancy desires.

CONTENTS

fish and seafood

STIR-FRIED PRAWNS IN AN AROMATIC TOMATO-CREAM SAUCE

Bhagari jhinga

Serves 4–5

INGREDIENTS

FOR THE SAUCE:

1 tablespoon tomato purée

¾ teaspoon salt

¼ teaspoon sugar

1 teaspoon store-bought garam masala

½ teaspoon ground roasted cumin seeds (p. 137)

⅛–¼ teaspoon chilli powder or to taste

3 tablespoons finely chopped green coriander

1 fresh, hot green chilli, finely chopped

1 tablespoon lemon juice

200 ml (7 fl oz) tinned coconut milk, well stirred, or single cream

FOR STIR-FRYING THE PRAWNS:

3 tablespoons vegetable oil

1 teaspoon black mustard seeds

3 cloves garlic, peeled and finely chopped

10–15 curry leaves (see above)

560 g (1¼ lb) medium-sized, uncooked, unpeeled prawns, peeled, deveined and washed (p. 134), then patted dry

One of the aromas that I find very refreshing in this particular dish is that of fresh curry leaves. I know that they are not always easy to find. Whenever you do come across them, get an extra supply and freeze them immediately in flat polythene bags. They hold up quite well. If you can get only dried curry leaves, mix them into the cream sauce instead of frying them with the prawns. If you cannot get them at all, just do without. The dish will still taste superb. To take fresh curry leaves off the stem, just pull along the stem with your thumb and first finger and they will come right off!

The sauce can be made several hours ahead of time and refrigerated. The prawns could be peeled, deveined, washed, patted dry and left covered in the refrigerator overnight, if necessary. The actual cooking takes just a few minutes. The dish is best served with rice.

Make the sauce: Put the tomato purée in a bowl. Add the salt, sugar, garam masala, ground roasted cumin seeds, chilli powder, green coriander, green chilli, lemon juice and 1 tablespoon water. Mix well. Slowly add the coconut milk or cream, mixing as you go. Set aside.

Stir-fry the prawns: Put the oil in a wok or frying pan and set over highish heat. When hot, put in the mustard seeds. As soon as the mustard seeds begin to pop – this takes just a few seconds – put in the garlic and curry leaves. Stir until the garlic turns medium-brown and put in the prawns. Stir until the prawns turn opaque most of the way through and put in the sauce. Turn the heat to medium and just heat the sauce through until it begins to simmer. By then the prawns should be completely opaque and cooked through. Turn off the heat.

PRAWNS STEAMED WITH MUSTARD SEEDS
Chingri bhapey

Serves 4

INGREDIENTS

1½ teaspoons black mustard seeds

1 tablespoon finely chopped onion

1 fresh, hot green chilli, finely chopped

¼ teaspoon ground turmeric

⅓ teaspoon salt

¼ teaspoon chilli powder

3 tablespoons mustard oil

450 g (1 lb) medium-sized, uncooked, unpeeled prawns, peeled, deveined and washed (p. 134) then drained

Very few people in the West associate the technique of gentle steaming with Indian cuisine. And yet, in many regions of India such as the East and the South, steaming is common and steaming utensils are standard in every kitchen. This simple, yet stunning, dish is a Bengali classic. Fish – in Bengal it can be pieces of hilsa, a kind of freshwater mackerel, or prawns – are put into a paste of crushed mustard seeds and mustard oil and left to steam briefly until the fish just turns opaque. The results are spectacular. The fish turns silken and the sauce created by the steam and the sweating fish is magically sweet and pungent. The dish is always eaten with plain rice.

Mustard oil is sold by Indian grocers. It is a good oil to know about. Pungent when raw, it turns comfortingly sweet when heated. Good-quality fish is essential here. Pieces of fresh haddock can be substituted for the prawn if you so desire. (See photograph overleaf.)

You may use one of two methods for steaming:

1 Put the bowl of prawns into a large saucepan. Pour boiling water into the pan so that it comes one-third of the way up the side of the bowl. Cover the saucepan and steam.

2 Put water in the bottom third of a large wok. Bring to the boil. Put a bamboo or perforated metal steaming-tray on top of the water. Place the bowl of prawns on the tray, cover the wok and steam.

Grind the mustard seeds coarsely in the container of a clean coffee grinder or other spice grinder. Put into a medium-sized stainless steel, ceramic or ovenproof-glass bowl. Add 1 tablespoon water and mix. Pour in the onion, green chilli, turmeric, salt, chilli powder and oil. Mix again. Put in the prawns and mix. Cover with foil and set aside for 10 minutes as you get your steaming equipment ready. Steam, covered, for about 10 minutes or until the prawns just turn opaque all the way through. Stir the prawns once after about 6 minutes, covering the bowl and steaming utensil afterwards.

CURRIED TUNA
Tuna ki kara

Serves 2–3

INGREDIENTS

1½ tablespoons vegetable oil

60 g (2 oz) onion, peeled and cut into very fine half-rings

1 clove garlic, peeled and very finely chopped

1 teaspoon curry powder

One 180 g (6 oz) tin good-quality tuna, packed in oil

½–1 fresh, hot green chilli, cut into very fine rounds

1 cm (½ inch) piece fresh ginger, peeled and cut into very fine slices, then into very fine strips

2–3 tablespoons chopped green coriander

Salt to taste

Freshly ground black pepper

This recipe, which is as good as it is simple, comes from Chun Kern, my friend from the Himalayan hills who now lives in the United States. You may eat this tuna in sandwiches, on toast, take it on picnics (I always do) or use it as a stuffing for 'turnover'-type patties made with store-bought puff pastry. It is excellent eaten plain with a variety of salads.

Use a good-quality tinned tuna packed in oil. I do not drain it as the oil prevents the tuna from drying out. Also, a good curry powder provides a useful short cut. I happen to like Bolst's hot curry powder, but use whichever one you like.

Put the oil in a non-stick frying pan and set over medium-high heat. When hot, put in the onion and garlic. Stir and fry until the onion turns brown at the edges. Put in the curry powder. Stir once or twice. Put in the tuna. Stir it around and break up any big lumps. Turn the heat to low. Add the green chilli, ginger and green coriander. Stir to mix. Check for salt, adding it if needed. Add a generous amount of black pepper. Mix well and turn off the heat. Serve hot, at room temperature or cold.

FISH IN A GREEN SAUCE
Haray masale ki macchi

Serves 2

INGREDIENTS

FOR MARINATING THE FISH:

2 good-sized steaks (about
675g/1½ lb) from a salmon or king
fish (see right)

Salt

Freshly ground black pepper

⅛ teaspoon ground turmeric

⅛ teaspoon chilli powder

FOR THE GREEN SAUCE:

3 tablespoons vegetable oil

85 g (3 oz) onions, peeled and
finely chopped

2 cloves garlic, peeled and finely
chopped

Teacup filled with finely chopped
green coriander

1 medium-sized tomato, finely
chopped

2–3 fresh, hot green chillies

1 teaspoon peeled, finely grated
fresh ginger

1 tablespoon lemon juice

⅛ teaspoon salt or to taste

⅛ teaspoon chilli powder

½ teaspoon store-bought garam
masala

You need steaks from a firm-fleshed fish here. King fish and salmon are ideal but cod would do as well. I season the fish first and let it marinate while I prepare the ingredients for the green sauce.

Rub the fish on both sides with a generous sprinkling of salt, lots of freshly ground pepper and the turmeric and chilli powder. Rub well and set aside. Put the oil in a non-stick frying pan and set over high heat. When hot, put in the fish and brown quickly on both sides without letting it cook through. Remove with a slotted spoon and set aside. Put in the onion and garlic. Stir and fry until the onion browns a bit. Put in the green coriander, tomato, green chillies, ginger, lemon juice and salt. Stir and cook over medium-high heat until the coriander and tomato have completely wilted. Spread the green sauce around in the frying pan and check the salt. Lay the fish over the top. Now spoon some green sauce over the fish. Sprinkle the chilli powder and garam masla over the top. Bring to a simmer. Cover, lower the heat and simmer gently for about 10 minutes.

FISH FILLETS IN A 'CURRY' SAUCE
'Curry' dar macchi

Serves 4–5

INGREDIENTS

900 g (2 lb) thick fish fillet or fillets (see right)

500 ml (18 fl oz) milk

1 teaspoon salt

Lots of freshly ground black pepper

½ teaspoon chilli powder

¼ teaspoon ground turmeric

5 tablespoons breadcrumbs (made from dried bread – home-made or store-bought)

60 g (2 oz) unsalted butter

4 tablespoons good curry powder

2 tablespoons plain flour

3 tablespoons finely chopped green coriander

2–3 teaspoons lemon juice

Bland white sauces were anathema to the Indian cooks who presided over Anglo-Indian households so they invariably added a few local seasonings in order to perk them up. Here is one such dish.

You may use any fish fillets – cod, haddock and halibut – although fillets of dark, oily fish, such as blue fish and mackerel are ideal. Get thick fillets if possible and, if the skin can be removed, so much the better.

Arrange a shelf in the upper third of the oven and pre-heat the oven to its highest temperature.

Spread the fish out in a somewhat deep dish. Combine the milk, salt, pepper, chilli powder and turmeric in a jug and pour over the fish. Set aside for 15 minutes. (Use this time to get all the remaining ingredients weighed, measured and chopped.) After the time is up, lift the fish out of the milk and dust both sides with the breadcrumbs, patting them on so that they adhere. Reserve the milk. Now put the fish in a shallow baking tray lined with foil. Dot with 30 g (1 oz) of the butter and bake for 15 minutes.

While the fish bakes, set the milk to heat. Melt the remaining 30 g (1 oz) butter in a small, heavy saucepan over medium-low heat. When it has melted and is bubbling, put in the curry powder. Stir for a minute. Now put in the flour. Stir for about 2 minutes. It should keep bubbling.

Take the saucepan off the heat and, using a whisk, beat in the hot milk. Now put the saucepan on medium-high heat and stir with the whisk until the sauce comes to a boil. Boil for a minute, whisking all the time. Add the green coriander and lemon juice. Stir to mix them in.

Put the fish on a serving plate or on individual plates. Pour the sauce over the top and serve immediately. Extra sauce, if there is any, may be served on the side.

GRILLED FISH STEAKS

Grill macchi

Serves 2–4

INGREDIENTS

675 g (1½ lb) fish steaks or thick pieces of filleted fish (see right)

Salt to taste

2 teaspoons freshly ground black pepper

½ teaspoon ground turmeric

¼ teaspoon chilli powder

1 teaspoon store-bought garam masala

3 tablespoons melted butter or vegetable oil

1 tablespoon grainy French mustard

4 tablespoons single cream

Lemon wedges

Normal fish steaks come with a central bone but sometimes chunky pieces of filleted haddock, salmon and fresh tuna also function as 'steaks'. With bone, 675 g (1½ lb) of fish steaks might serve just two people. Without the bone, they would serve four. You can use anything from cod, halibut and haddock to fresh tuna, swordfish and salmon.

Spread the fish steaks out in a single layer. Sprinkle adequately on both sides with salt and then with the black pepper, turmeric, chilli powder and garam masala. Pat the spices in and set aside for 15 minutes.

Pre-heat the grill.

Dribble half the melted butter or oil over one side of the fish pieces and grill them about 10 cm (4 inches) from the source of heat for 2–3 minutes or until they are just starting to brown. Mix the mustard and cream and brush the fish with half of that mixture. Grill for another 2 minutes or so or until the fish is golden-brown. Turn the pieces over and repeat the process, first with a brushing of butter or oil and then with the remaining mustard-cream mixture. Serve hot with the lemon wedges.

FRIED FISH STEAKS
Tali macchi

Serves 3

INGREDIENTS

3 medium-sized cod steaks
(about 630 g/1 lb 6 oz)

⅓–½ teaspoon salt

½–¾ teaspoon freshly ground black
pepper

¼ teaspoon ground turmeric

¼ teaspoon chilli powder or to taste

½ teaspoon store-bought garam
masala

1 tablespoon plain flour

4 tablespoons vegetable oil

3 lemon wedges

Cod steaks with bone are ideal for this very satisfying dish although any fish steaks may be used. It may be served as part of an Indian meal or Western-style with boiled potatoes and a salad or cooked vegetable.

Lay the fish pieces out in a single layer on a big plate. Dust evenly on both sides with the salt, black pepper, turmeric, chilli powder and garam masala. Rub the spices in. Now dust both sides with the flour and let the steaks sit for 10–15 minutes.

Put the oil in a large frying pan and set over medium-high heat. When hot, put in the steaks in a single layer. When one side turns golden-brown, turn the fish pieces over carefully and brown the second side as well. The fish is done when it is just cooked through. Remove with a slotted spatula and serve with the lemon wedges.

SPICY GRILLED FISH

Masaledar macchi

Serves 2–3

INGREDIENTS

560 g (1¼ lb) fish such as a salmon trout, trout or small salmon, scaled, cleaned and left whole

Salt

3 tablespoons lemon juice

60 g (2 oz) onion, peeled and coarsely chopped

2 cloves garlic, peeled and coarsely chopped

2.5 cm (1 inch) piece fresh ginger

1 fresh, hot green chilli, sliced

¼ teaspoon ground turmeric

1 teaspoon store-bought garam masala

¼ teaspoon chilli powder

175 ml (6 fl oz) tinned coconut milk, well stirred

A little vegetable oil

Fish is grilled all along India's coastline, using a variety of marinades and basting sauces. Sometimes the grilling is done over rice straw, at other times over smouldering coconut husks. In the north, fish is often grilled – quick-baked might be a better description – in a tandoor. I have used my indoor grill here but you could also grill outdoors over charcoal.

What helps the grilling enormously is a hinged, double-racked 'holder'. The fish is placed securely inside it. It can then be turned and basted with ease. Such racks are sold by shops specializing in kitchen equipment. If you cannot find one, just oil your grill rack well and lay your fish directly on it.

Wash the fish well and pat dry. Cut 3–4 deep, diagonal slits across both sides of the fish. Rub with ½ teaspoon salt and 1 tablespoon of the lemon juice. Set aside as you make the marinade.

Combine the remaining lemon juice, ¼ teaspoon salt, onion, garlic, ginger, green chilli, turmeric, garam masala and chilli powder in the container of an electric blender and blend until smooth. Empty the paste into a shallow dish large enough to hold the fish. Add the coconut milk and mix. Now put the fish into the dish and rub with the marinade. Leave for 5–10 minutes. Meanwhile, pre-heat your indoor grill and oil your grilling rack with a little vegetable oil. The rack should be placed about 15 cm (6 inches) from the source of heat.

Lift the fish out of the marinade and place it in (or on) the rack. Grill for about 25 minutes, turning the fish every 5 minutes and basting frequently with the marinade. If you do not have a hinged rack, turn only once, midway through the cooking, using the flat side of a large chef's knife. If the fish is browning too fast, distance it some more from the source of heat. Do not baste towards the end to allow the fish to form a crust.

SQUID OR SCALLOPS IN A SPINACH-TOMATO CURRY SAUCE

Samundar ki kari

Serves 4

INGREDIENTS

½ teaspoon chilli powder

½ teaspoon ground turmeric

1 teaspoon ground cumin

1 teaspon ground coriander

1⅛ teaspoons salt

Freshly ground black pepper

1 teaspoon grainy French mustard

3 tablespoons vegetable oil

1 teaspoon black or yellow mustard seeds

If you are rushed, it is best to buy cleaned squid. Frozen squid, sold by Chinese grocers, usually comes all cleaned and is totally acceptable. Directions for cleaning fresh squid are on p. 134. Once cleaned, the squid's tubular body should be cut into 5 mm (¼ inch) wide rings. The head area and tentacles may be left whole or halved. Scallops, of course, are sold ready for cooking!

This dish may be eaten with rice or, oddly enough, with noodles. It is superb for entertaining. You could, if you like, make it with peeled prawns.

3–4 cloves garlic, peeled and finely chopped

1 cm (½ inch) piece fresh ginger, peeled and finely chopped

150 ml (5 fl oz) tinned chopped tomatoes (or lightly drained, tinned whole tomatoes, finely chopped)

115 g (4 oz) fresh spinach, cut, crossways, into fine strips

560 g (1¼ lb) cleaned, sliced squid (see opposite) or whole scallops

120 ml (4 fl oz) tinned coconut milk, well-stirred, or single cream

Combine the chilli powder, turmeric, cumin, coriander, salt, black pepper, French mustard and 2 tablespoons water in a small bowl. Mix.

Put the oil in a large, non-stick frying pan and set over high heat. When hot, put in the whole mustard seeds. As soon as they begin to pop – a matter of seconds – put in the garlic and ginger. Stir and fry until the garlic turns a light brown. Add the spice paste. Stir and fry for 15 seconds. Put in the tomatoes and spinach. Stir and cook for a minute. Add 250 ml (8 fl oz) water and bring to a simmer. Simmer, uncovered, on low heat for 10 minutes. Put in the squid or scallops. Turn the heat to high. Stir and cook until the squid or scallops just turn opaque. This will happen quite fast. Put in the coconut milk or cream and bring to a simmer. Stir and simmer for half a minute. Turn off the heat.

Legumes and vegetables are the heart of traditional Indian meals. Most legumes cook slowly – and for a long time. I have included only those that can be prepared fast, such as red lentils and whole green lentils and even tinned chickpeas that just need dressing up. As for vegetables, nearly all cook quickly. I have chosen recipes that are quite simple to put together.

CONTENTS

legumes and
vegetables
legumes and
vegetables
legumes and
vegetables
legumes and
vegetables
legumes and
vegetables
legumes and
vegetables

CHICKPEAS COOKED IN TEA

Dhabay kay chanay

Serves 4–5

INGREDIENTS

Two 500 g (19 oz) tins chickpeas

4 tablespoons vegetable oil

A generous pinch of ground asafetida

1 teaspoon cumin seeds

180 g (6 oz) onions, peeled and chopped

3 cloves garlic, peeled and finely chopped

4 tablespoons tinned chopped tomatoes

2 teaspoons peeled, finely grated ginger

Cooked in tea? You might well ask! This is the trick that all the vendors at truck stops use to give their chickpeas a traditional dark appearance. The tea – left-over tea may be used here – leaves no after-taste. It just alters the colour of the chickpeas.

For speed, I have used tinned chickpeas. As they are already cooked, they need just 10 minutes of gentle simmering to absorb the flavourings. I have also used tinned chopped tomatoes. If you wish to substitute fresh ones, chop them very finely and use eight tablespoons instead of four.

This chickpea dish may be served with store-bought pitta bread, a yoghurt relish and some pickles or salad. It could also be part of a more elaborate meal with meat or chicken, a green vegetable and rice.

300 ml (10 fl oz) prepared tea (use a fairly plain one – water may be substituted)

1–2 fresh, hot green chillies, cut into very fine rounds

1 teaspoon salt

2 teaspoons ground roasted cumin seeds (p. 137)

1 teaspoon store-bought garam masala

3–4 tablespoons coarsely chopped green coriander

1 tablespoon lemon juice

Drain the chickpeas. Rinse them gently with fresh water. Drain again.

Put the oil in a wide pan and set over medium-high heat. When hot, put in the asafetida. Let it sizzle for a second. Now put in the cumin seeds and let them sizzle for about 15 seconds. Put in the onions. Stir and fry until the onions turn quite brown at the edges. Put in the garlic and let it turn golden, stirring as this happens. Now put in the tomatoes. Stir and cook them until they turn dark and thick. Add the ginger and give a few good stirs. Now put in the chickpeas and all the remaining ingredients. Bring to a simmer. Turn the heat to low and simmer, uncovered, for about 10 minutes, stirring gently now and then. Taste for balance of flavours and make necessary adjustments.

SPINACH WITH GINGER AND GREEN CHILLIES

Saag bhaji

Serves 4

INGREDIENTS

2 cm (1 inch) piece fresh ginger, peeled

3 tablespoons vegetable oil

500 g (18 oz) trimmed, washed spinach

2–3 fresh, hot green chillies, finely chopped

About ½ teaspoon salt

½ teaspoon store-bought garam masala

¼ teaspoon sugar

⅛ teaspoon chilli powder

Indians tend to eat a lot of greens, sometimes a single variety by itself, sometimes mixed with other leaves. The most commonly available of all greens in the West is spinach and that is what I have used here. I keep the leaves whole, but if they are very large you might need to chop them coarsely.

Cut the ginger, crossways, into very thick slices. Stacking a few slices at a time together, cut them into very fine slivers.

Put the oil in a wok or large, wide pan and set over high heat. When very hot, put in the ginger. Stir until the ginger starts to brown. Put in the spinach and chillies. Stir and cook until the spinach has wilted completely. Add the remaining ingredients. Stir and cook for another 5 minutes.

STIR-FRIED GREEN CABBAGE WITH FENNEL SEEDS

Bhuni bandh gobi

Serves 4

INGREDIENTS

675 g (1½ lb) green cabbage (half a big head)

4 tablespoons vegetable oil

¾ teaspoon cumin seeds

½ teaspoon fennel seeds

1 teaspoon sesame seeds

200 g (7 oz) onions, peeled and cut, lengthways, into fine half-rings

1 teaspoon salt

⅛–¼ teaspoon chilli powder

1 tablespoon lemon juice

½ teaspoon store-bought garam masala

The cabbage and onions get nicely browned here and taste gloriously of fennel. You could easily serve this with Western-style sausages, hams, pork chops or any kind of roast pork meat, or try it with roast lamb or even duck and venison.

Remove the coarse outer leaves of the cabbage. If you have a cabbage half, cut it in half again, lengthways, and then core the sections. Now cut each section, lengthways, into very fine, long shreds. A bread knife is ideal for this. (You could also use a food processor.)

Put the oil in a wide, preferably non-stick, pan and set over highish heat. When hot, put in the cumin, fennel and sesame seeds. As soon as the sesame seeds begin to pop, put in the onions. Stir and fry for 3–4 minutes or until the onions have browned a bit. Put in the cabbage. Stir and fry for about 6 minutes or until the cabbage too has browned somewhat. Now put in the salt and chilli powder. Turn the heat down to medium-low and cook, stirring now and then, for another 7–8 minutes or until the onions appear caramelized and soft. Add the lemon juice and garam masala. Stir to mix.

CAULIFLOWER WITH GINGER, GARLIC AND GREEN CHILLIES

Sookhi gobi

Serves 3–4

INGREDIENTS

3 tablespoons vegetable oil

½ teaspoon cumin seeds

½ teaspoon yellow mustard seeds

3 cloves garlic, peeled and finely chopped

2.5 cm (1 inch) piece fresh ginger, peeled and cut into fine shreds

450 g (1 lb) cauliflower florets

1–3 fresh, hot green chillies

¾ teaspoon salt

Freshly ground black pepper

½ teaspoon store-bought garam masala

⅛ teaspoon chilli powder or to taste

A simple, everyday dish. The special taste comes from allowing the florets to brown slightly. Do not cut them too small or they might fall apart. (See photograph overleaf.)

Put the oil in a wok and set over highish heat. When hot, put in the cumin and mustard seeds. As soon as the mustard seeds begin to pop – this just takes a few seconds – put in the garlic, ginger, cauliflower and green chillies, all at the same time. Stir and fry for about 5–7 minutes or until the cauliflower has turned somewhat brown. Now put in the salt, black pepper, garam masala and chilli powder and give the florets a good toss. Put in 4 tablespoons water and cover the wok immediately. Cook for 2 minutes more and serve immediately.

CABBAGE STIR-FRIED WITH RED PEPPER PASTE

Sala lobak

Serves 4

INGREDIENTS

450 g (1 lb) bok choi, other cabbage, cabbage greens or spring greens

100 g (4 oz) red pepper

50 g (2 oz) shallots or onions

2 large cloves garlic

½ teaspoon shrimp or anchovy paste (optional)

¼ teaspoon chilli powder

6 tablespoons vegetable oil

½ teaspoon salt

Only the dark, outer leaves of the cabbage were originally included in this recipe but I often add some of the inner cabbage together with a small amount of shrimp or anchovy paste.

Wash the cabbage leaves and drain. Stacking several of them together, cut them crossways into long, fine, 3 mm (⅛ inch) wide shreds.

Core and deseed the red pepper, then chop coarsely. Peel and coarsely chop the shallots and garlic. Put the red pepper, shallots, garlic, shrimp paste, chilli powder and 3 tablespoons water in an electric blender. Blend until a coarse paste results – it should not be too smooth.

Set a wok over a high heat. When hot, add the oil. Once the oil is hot, put in the spice paste. Stir and fry for about 5 minutes or until the oil separates and the mixture is dark red in colour.

Add the cabbage and salt and cook, stirring, for 30 seconds. Cover tightly, turn the heat to medium-low and cook for 8–10 minutes or until the cabbage is just cooked. (No water should be needed, but check after 5–6 minutes and add a little if the mixture appears dry.) Turn into a warmed dish and serve at once.

CAULIFLOWER AND CARROTS WITH A COCONUT DRESSING

Gudangan

Serves 4

You may serve this dish hot, at room tempearture, or cold, though I feel that it is best to mix the dressing in while the vegetables are still hot.

INGREDIENTS

50 g (2 oz) fresh coconut, or 25 g (1 oz) unsweetened desiccated coconut

425 g (15 oz) cauliflower florets

100 g (4 oz) carrots

50 g (2 oz) red pepper

1 clove garlic

4 teaspoons lime or lemon juice

1 teaspoon dark brown sugar

½ teaspoon chilli powder

Salt

If you are using fresh coconut, grate it finely. If using desiccated coconut, soak it in 4 tablespoons of boiling water or 30 minutes; most of the water will be absorbed.

Cut the cauliflower into slim delicate florets – no wider than 2.5 cm (1 inch), with stems no longer than 5 cm (2 inches). Peel the carrots and cut into 5 cm (2 inch) lengths. Quarter the thick pieces lengthways; halve the thinner pointed ends.

Deseed and coarsely chop the red pepper. Peel and chop the garlic. In an electric blender combine the red pepper, garlic, lime juice, sugar, chilli powder and ½ teaspoon salt. Blend until smooth. Taste the dressing and add a little more salt if required.

Bring a large pan of salted water to a rolling boil. Add the cauliflower and carrots and boil rapidly for several minutes or until the vegetables are just tender but still retain a hint of crispness.

Drain them quickly and turn into a serving bowl. Add the dressing and toss to mix. Sprinkle in the coconut and toss the vegetables again. Serve immediately, or allow to cool.

RED LENTILS 'TARKA'
Masoor dal

Serves 6–8

INGREDIENTS

340 g (12 oz) red lentils (masoor dal)

½ teaspoon ground turmeric

1¼–1½ teaspoons salt

3 tablespoons vegetable oil or ghee

A generous pinch of ground asafetida

1 teaspoon cumin seeds

3–5 dried, hot red chillies

Indians tend to eat protein-rich legumes with many everyday meals. Often, these are prepared with just a flavouring, or 'tarka', of whole cumin seeds, asafetida and whole chillies popped in hot oil or ghee. Mustard seeds and a choice of garlic, curry leaves, onions, even tomatoes may be added to this 'tarka'. I have used red lentils here, partly because they are sold by all health food shops and make the shopping very easy but mainly because they cook faster than most other traditional dals (split peas). Serve this dish with plain rice and a simple meat or vegetable. Yoghurt relishes and pickles make good accompaniments.

Pick over the lentils and wash in several changes of water. Drain. Put in a heavy saucepan. Add 1.2 litres (2 pints) water and the turmeric. Stir and bring to a simmer. (Do not let it boil over.) Cover in such a way as to leave the lid just very slightly ajar, turn the heat to low and simmer gently for 35–40 minutes or until tender. Stir a few times during the cooking. Add the salt and mix. Leave covered, on very low heat, as you do the next step.

Put the oil in a small frying pan and set over highish heat. When hot, put in the asafetida then, a second later, the cumin seeds. Let the cumin seeds sizzle for a few seconds. Put in the red chillies. As soon as they turn dark red (this takes just a few seconds), lift up the lid of the lentil pan and pour in the contents of the frying pan, oil as well as spices. Cover the saucepan immediately to trap the aromas.

WHOLE GREEN LENTILS WITH GREEN CORIANDER AND MINT

Sabut peeli massoor

Serves 4

INGREDIENTS

3 tablespoons vegetable oil

½ teaspoon cumin seeds

½ teaspoon black or yellow mustard seeds

A pinch of ground asafetida (optional)

1–3 dried, hot red chillies

115 g (4 oz) onions, peeled and cut into fine half-rings

2 cloves garlic, peeled and chopped

1 medium-sized tomato, chopped

180 g (6 oz) whole green lentils

¾ teaspoon salt

1 teaspoon ground coriander

½ teacup chopped green coriander

½ teacup chopped fresh mint

For speed, I use a pressure-cooker although you could cook the lentils in an ordinary saucepan for 50–60 minutes. You would need to increase the water by 300 ml (10 fl oz). If you cannot get fresh mint, use more green coriander.

Put the oil in a pressure-cooker and set over highish heat. When hot, put in the cumin and mustard seeds. As soon as the mustard seeds begin to pop – this takes just a few seconds – put in the asafetida and the red chillies. Stir once. Put in the onions, garlic and tomato. Stir for about 2 minutes or until the onions brown a bit. Now put in the lentils, 800 ml (1 pint 7 fl oz) water, salt, ground coriander, green coriander and mint. Stir and bring to a simmer. Cover, turn the heat to high and bring up to pressure. Turn the heat down to low and cook at full pressure for 15 minutes. Take off the heat, reduce the pressure with cool water and serve.

MUSHROOM CURRY

Shorvedar khumbi

Serves 4

I have used ordinary white mushrooms here but you may make this with almost any seasonal mushrooms. Whichever kind you get, cut them into large, chunky pieces so they do not get lost in the sauce.

INGREDIENTS

4 cm (1½ inch) piece fresh ginger, peeled and chopped

115 g (4 oz) onions, peeled and chopped

3 cloves garlic, peeled and chopped

450 g (1 lb) large mushrooms

6 tablespoons vegetable oil

3 tablespoons natural yoghurt

1 teaspoon tomato purée

2 teaspoons ground coriander

¾ teaspoon salt

⅛ – ¼ teaspoon chilli powder

2 tablespoons chopped green coriander

Put the ginger, onion and garlic into the container of an electric blender along with 3 tablespoons water and blend until smooth.

Wipe the mushrooms with a damp cloth and cut them into halves or quarters, depending upon size.

Put 3 tablespoons of the oil in a non-stick frying pan and set over high heat. When hot, put in the mushrooms. Stir and fry for 2–3 minutes or until the mushrooms have lost their raw look. Empty the contents of the pan into a bowl. Wipe the pan.

Put the remaining 3 tablespoons oil into the pan and set over high heat. When hot, put in the paste from the blender. Stir and fry for 3–4 minutes until it starts turning brown. Add 1 tablespoon of the yoghurt and fry for 30 seconds. Add another tablespoon of the yoghurt and fry for 30 seconds. Do this a third time. Now put in the tomato purée and fry for 30 seconds. Put in the ground coriander and stir once or twice. Now put in 300 ml (10 fl oz) water, the mushrooms and their juices, salt and chilli powder. Stir and bring to a simmer. Turn the heat to low and simmer for 5 minutes. Sprinkle the green coriander over the top before serving.

GREEN BEANS WITH MUSHROOMS

Sem aur khumbi

Serves 4

A hearty dish that may be served as part of an all-vegetarian meal or with any meat, poultry or fish.

INGREDIENTS

5 tablespoons vegetable oil

¾ teaspoon cumin seeds

1 medium-sized onion, peeled and cut into fine half-rings

2.5 cm (1 inch) piece fresh ginger, peeled and cut into slivers

5 cloves garlic, peeled and chopped

225 g (8 oz) fresh mushrooms, thickly sliced

450 g (1 lb) green beans, trimmed and cut into 5 cm (2 inch) segments

2 teaspoons ground coriander

1½ teaspoons ground cumin

½ teaspoon ground turmeric

¾ teaspoon store-bought garam masala

¾ teaspoon chilli powder

1 teaspoon salt

1 medium-sized tomato, coarsely chopped

Put the oil in a wide pan and set over medium-high heat. When hot, put in the cumin seeds. As soon as the seeds begin to sizzle, put in the onion. Stir and fry until the onion browns. Put in the ginger and garlic. Stir until the garlic starts to brown. Put in the mushrooms. Stir and fry for 2 minutes. Put in the beans, ground coriander, ground cumin, turmeric, garam masala, chilli powder, salt, tomato and 120 ml (4 fl oz) water. Bring to a boil. Cover, lower the heat and simmer for 15 minutes. Remove the cover, raise the heat and boil most of the liquid away, stirring gently as you do so.

GENTLY STEWED BEETROOTS

Taridar chukandar

Serves 4–6

INGREDIENTS

900 g (2 lb) raw beetroots without stems and leaves

3 tablespoons vegetable oil

1 teaspoon cumin seeds

1 bay leaf

250 ml (8 fl oz) tinned chopped tomatoes (or lightly drained tinned whole tomatoes)

1 teaspoon ground cumin

1 teaspoon ground coriander

¼ teaspoon ground turmeric

¼ teaspoon chilli powder

¾ teaspoon salt

Any beetroots may be used for this stew-like dish. My own favourite happens to be chioggia, a very early Italian variety. These beetroots are small and sweet, with radish-red skin and striated red and pale yellow flesh. I do not mean to sound like a garden catalogue, but these are certainly worth knowing about, if not growing. Mine are supplied by a local farmer.

Peel the beetroots and cut them in 2.5 cm (1 inch) chunks.

Put the oil in a wide, medium-sized pan and set over high heat. When hot, put in the cumin seeds and bay leaf. As soon as the bay leaf darkens slightly – this just takes seconds – put in the tomatoes, ground cumin, ground coriander, turmeric, chilli powder, beetroots, salt and 350 ml (12 fl oz) water. Stir and bring to a boil. Cover, turn the heat to low and simmer for 30–40 minutes or until the beetroots are tender.

GREEN PEAS IN A CREAMY SAUCE

Matar makhani

Serves 5–6

INGREDIENTS

¼ teaspoon sugar

½ teaspoon ground cumin

½ teaspoon home-made garam masala (p. 138)

¾ teaspoon salt

¼–½ teaspoon chilli powder

1 tablespoon tomato purée

175 ml (6 fl oz) single cream

1 tablespoon lemon juice

2 tablespoons chopped green coriander

1 fresh, hot green chilli, finely chopped

3 tablespoons vegetable oil

½ teaspoon cumin seeds

½ teaspoon black or yellow mustard seeds

Two 285 g (10 oz) packets frozen peas, completely defrosted under warm water and drained

This is a recipe where frozen peas can be used to great advantage. The sauce takes just minutes to put together and may be made up to a day in advance and refrigerated, if you so prefer. This dish may be served with all Indian meals. It also goes well with lamb and pork roasts.

Combine the sugar, ground cumin, garam masala, salt, chilli powder and tomato purée. Slowly add 2 tablespoons water, mixing as you go. Add the cream slowly and mix. Put in the lemon juice, green coriander and green chilli. Mix again and set this cream sauce aside.

Put the oil in a large frying pan and set over medium-high heat. When hot, put in the cumin and mustard seeds. As soon as the mustard seeds begin to pop – this just takes a few seconds – put in the peas. Stir and fry the peas for 30 seconds. Put in the cream sauce. Cook on high heat for about 1½–2 minutes or until the sauce has thickened, stirring gently as you do so.

SIMPLY GRILLED TOMATOES

Grilled timatar

Serves 2–4

INGREDIENTS

500–560 g (18–20 oz) tomatoes

¼ teaspoon salt

Freshly ground black pepper

¼ teaspoon store-bought garam masala

¼ teaspoon ground cumin

A generous pinch of chilli powder

2 teaspoons lemon juice

2 teaspoons butter or olive oil (optional)

Sweet, juicy summer tomatoes are just perfect cooked this way. You will want to try them with your fried eggs as well as many of the chicken and fish dishes in this book.

I like to use two large tomatoes but any size will do.

Pre-heat the grill.

Cut the tomatoes in halves crossways. Sprinkle the salt, black pepper, garam masala, cumin and chilli powder over the cut surfaces and rub the spices in. Sprinkle the lemon juice on top and rub that in as well. Place under the hot grill, about 10 cm (4 inches) from the source of heat and grill until the top is browned and the tomatoes are slightly limp. Dot with butter or dribble some oil over the top if you like.

NEW POTATOES WITH CUMIN

Zeera aloo

Serves 4–6

INGREDIENTS

900 g (2 lb) new potatoes

Salt

2½ tablespoons vegetable oil

1 teaspoon cumin seeds

1 teaspoon ground cumin

½ teaspoon store-bought garam masala

⅛–¼ teaspoon chilli powder

2–3 tablespoons chopped green coriander

Here is one of my favourite ways of preparing new potatoes, Indian-style. You may serve them with an Indian meal or, if you like, with Western dishes – anything from roasts to sausages. They are particularly good with my 'Hamburger' Kebabs (p. 24).

Scrub the potatoes and put them in a saucepan. Cover with water to come about 2.5 cm (1 inch) above the potatoes. Add 1 tablespoon salt to the water and bring to a boil. Cover. Boil until the potatoes are just tender. Drain and peel.

Put the oil in a large frying pan and set over medium-high heat. When hot, put in the cumin seeds. Let the seeds sizzle for a few seconds. Now put in the potatoes. Turn the heat down to medium. Brown the potatoes lightly on all sides. Turn the heat to low and add ¼ teaspoon salt and the ground cumin, garam masala and chilli powder. Cook, stirring, for a minute. Add the green coriander just before serving and toss to mix.

INDIAN MASHED POTATOES

Mash aloo

Serves 4–6

INGREDIENTS

1 kg (2¼ lb) potatoes, peeled and cut into large chunks

175–200 ml (6–7 fl oz) hot milk

60–85 g (2–3 oz) butter, cut into pieces

1¼ teaspoons salt or to taste

Freshly ground black pepper

1 fresh, hot green chilli, finely chopped

3 tablespoons finely chopped green coriander

1 teaspoon store-bought garam masala

A pinch of chilli powder

1½ tablespoons lemon juice

Indians are always using spicy mashed potatoes to make potato patties and deep-fried potato balls, so it occurred to me that the same mixture could be served plain – and that it would be wonderful with all manner of fish, poultry and meat dishes. I tried it out, it was wonderful and here it is.

Boil the potatoes with water to cover. When they are tender – this will take 15–20 minutes – drain and mash them with the back of a fork or a potato masher. Now add the hot milk and butter and beat with a whisk or a fork. Add all the remaining ingredients and mix well.

TIP

The best way to keep mashed potatoes hot if you are not eating them right away is in a covered double-boiler.

TURNIPS WITH CUMIN
Shorvedar shaljam

Serves 4

INGREDIENTS

450 g (1 lb) medium-sized turnips
(about 5)

2 tablespoons chickpea flour
(also called gram flour or besan)

5 tinned plum tomatoes, well
chopped, plus 6 tablespoons juice
from the tin

2 tablespoons vegetable oil

½ teaspoon cumin seeds

2–3 hot, dried red chillies

⅛ teaspoon ground turmeric

¾ teaspoon salt

To this simple stew, you may, if you like, add other vegetables such as potatoes, peas, carrots or green beans. Serve it with rice or a bread.

Turnips can have a rather thick skin. You should peel all of it away so that you will not be left with a coarse outer layer.

Peel the turnips and quarter them lengthways.

Put the chickpea flour in a bowl. Slowly add 2 tablespoons water, breaking up lumps as you go. Add the tinned tomatoes, the juice from the tin and another 4 tablespoons water. Set aside.

Put the oil in a medium-sized pan and set over medium-high heat. When hot, put in the cumin seeds. Stir once or twice and put in the red chillies. Stir once and put in the turnips and turmeric. Stir a few times and put in 120 ml (4 fl oz) water, the chickpea flour paste and salt. Stir and bring to a boil. Cover, turn the heat to low and simmer for 15–20 minutes or until the turnips are tender.

Here are a few basic recipes to set you on your way. Plain rice cooks quickly anyway. If you add some herbs, spices or vegetables, the cooking time may increase by a few minutes. Breads are more of a problem as the dough needs to rest and then the breads have to be rolled out. But the bread I have included here cooks in less than a minute!

These days, good Indian and Middle Eastern breads are sold by many supermarkets and take-aways. To make your life easier, you can always buy these to eat with your delicious home-made chickpeas or chicken or lamb.

CONTENTS

bread and rice

bread and rice

bread and rice

bread and rice

bread and rice

bread and rice

bread and rice

bread and rice

bread and rice

bread and rice

DEEP-FRIED PUFFY BREADS

Poori

Serves 3–4

INGREDIENTS

225 g (8 oz) chapati flour or a mixture of 115 g (4 oz) sieved wheatmeal flour and 115 g (4 oz) plain white flour

½ teaspoon salt

2 tablespoons vegetable oil plus more for deep-frying

About 100–200 ml (3½–4 fl oz) milk or water

Pooris, for me, are the easiest of Indian breads and the first ones I teach in my cooking classes. Hence their inclusion in this chapter. These days you can always buy ready-made naans, pitta breads and even chapatis from supermarkets or take-aways. But pooris you do have to make yourself. They are quite heavenly when freshly prepared.

Chapati flour is sold by all Indian grocers. If you wish to measure the flour in volume, you will need to fill a measuring jug up to the 475 ml (16 fl oz) level. (See photograph overleaf.)

Put the flour in a bowl. Add the salt and mix it in. Dribble the 2 tablespoons oil over the top and rub it into the flour with your fingers. Slowly add the milk or water to form a medium-soft ball of dough. Knead the dough for 10 minutes or until smooth. Form a smooth ball, rub it with a little oil and set it aside, covered, for 15–30 minutes.

Just before eating, put enough oil for deep-frying into a wok or deep frying pan and set over medium heat. As it heats, divide the ball of dough into 12 balls. Roll one ball out into a 13 cm (5 inch) round. Keep it covered with cling film. Roll out all the pooris this way and keep them covered. When the oil is very hot, lay one poori carefully over the surface of the oil without letting it fold up. It should sizzle immediately. Using the back of a slotted spoon, push the poori gently into the oil with quick strokes. it should puff up in seconds. Turn the poori over and cook on the second side for a few seconds. Remove with a slotted spoon and keep on a large plate lined with paper towels. Make all the pooris this way and eat immediately.

PLAIN RICE

Saaday chaaval

Serves 4–6

INGREDIENTS

Long grain rice measured to the
450 ml (15 fl oz) level in a
measuring jug

1 teaspoon salt, optional

Put the rice in a bowl and wash well in several changes of water. Drain
thoroughly.

In a heavy-bottomed saucepan, combine the rice, salt and 675 ml (22 fl oz)
water. Bring to a boil. Cover tightly, turn the heat to very, very low and cook
for 25 minutes.

TURMERIC RICE
Peelay chaaval

Serves 4–6

This yellow, lightly seasoned rice may be served with almost any Indian meal. (See photograph overleaf.)

INGREDIENTS

Basmati rice measured to the 450 ml (15 fl oz) level in a measuring jug

3 tablespoons vegetable oil

3 cloves

1 bay leaf

4 cardamom pods

2.5 cm (1 inch) cinnamon stick

2 cloves garlic, peeled and finely chopped

¼ teaspoon ground turmeric

1 teaspooon salt

2 tablespoons finely sliced chives or the green part of spring onions

Put the rice in a bowl and wash well in several changes of water. Drain and leave in a strainer set over a bowl.

Put the oil in a heavy saucepan and set over medium-high heat. When hot, put in the cloves, bay leaf, cardamom pods and cinnamon. Stir once or twice and put in the garlic. As soon as the garlic turns medium-brown, put in the rice, turmeric and salt. Stir gently for a minute. Now put in 675 ml (22 fl oz) water and bring to a boil. Cover tightly, turn the heat down to very, very low and cook for 25 minutes.

RICE WITH MUSHROOMS AND MUSTARD SEEDS

Khumbi chaaval

Serves 4–5

Almost any variety of fresh, seasonal mushrooms may be used here. Ordinary white ones also work perfectly well.

INGREDIENTS

Long grain rice measured to the 450 ml (15 fl oz) level in a measuring jug

3 tablespoons vegetable oil

½ teaspoon cumin seeds

½ teaspoon black or yellow mustard seeds

30 g (1 oz) onion, peeled and cut into fine half-rings

10 medium-sized mushrooms, sliced lengthways

675 ml (22 fl oz) chicken stock or water

Salt

Put the rice in a bowl and wash well in several changes of water. Drain and leave in a strainer set over a bowl.

Put the oil in a heavy saucepan and set over medium-high heat. When hot, put in the cumin and mustard seeds. As soon as the mustard seeds begin to pop – this takes just a few seconds – put in the onion. Stir and fry until the onion browns a little. Put in the mushrooms and stir for a minute. Now put in the drained rice and stir for a minute. Put in the stock and about ½ teaspoon salt if your stock is salted, 1 teaspoon salt if you are using water or unsalted stock. Bring to a boil. Cover tightly, turn the heat to very, very low and cook for 25 minutes.

RICE WITH PEAS AND DILL

Matar aur sooay ka pullao

Serves 5–6

This dish is just as good for the family as it is for dinner guests.

INGREDIENTS

Basmati rice measured to the 450 ml (15 fl oz) level in a measuring jug

3 tablespoons vegetable oil

3 cloves

4 cardamom pods

1 small onion, peeled and cut into fine half-rings

1 teaspoon salt

1 teaspoon store-bought or home-made garam masala (p. 138)

4 tablespoons finely chopped fresh dill or 1½ tablespoons dried dill

675 ml (22 fl oz) chicken stock (use water as a substitute)

1 teaspoon salt if using unsalted stock or water

140 g (5 oz) fresh or frozen peas, cooked for just 2 minutes in boiling water

Put the rice in a bowl and wash well in several changes of water. Drain and leave in a strainer set over a bowl.

Put the oil in a heavy saucepan and set over medium-high heat. When hot, put in the cloves and cardamom pods. Stir for a few seconds. Put in the onion. Stir until the onion is brown. Put in the rice, salt, garam masala and dill. Stir for a minute. Now put in the stock and the salt, if needed, and bring to a boil. Cover very tightly, turn the heat to very, very low and leave to cook for 20 minutes. Put in the peas. Cook for another 5–7 minutes. Stir gently before serving.

India has a whole world of little salads, relishes, chutneys and pickles. No meal is considered complete without at least one such offering to perk it up. Not only do these offerings add tiny bits of concentrated flavour to a meal, they also add vitamins. They are taken for granted and appear without being asked for. Sometimes they can be as simple as finely sliced red onions and tomatoes sprinked with salt, pepper and lemon juice, or they can be pickles that take a few days to mature.

Every home has its own mini-tradition of preparing carrot pickle with brown sugar, for example, or putting curry leaves into mango pickle or making mango chutney with a particular spice combination. I have included one very special mango chutney here: Fresh Green Mango Chutney (p. 118). It was made by my mother in the hot summer months and is quite extraordinary. It is also quick and easy to prepare!

CONTENTS

salads, relishes, chutneys and pickles

salads, relishes, chutneys and pickles

salads, relishes, chutneys and pickles

salads, relishes, chutneys and pickles

YOGHURT WITH CARROT AND SULTANAS

Gajar aur kishmish ka raita

Serves 4

INGREDIENTS

300 ml (10 fl oz) natural yoghurt

½ teaspoon sugar

¼ teaspoon salt

¼ teaspoon chilli powder

1 medium-sized carrot, peeled and coarsely grated

1 tablespoon vegetable oil

¼ teaspoon cumin seeds

¼ teaspoon black or yellow mustard seeds

2 tablespoons sultanas

The taste of this takes me back to the hundreds of festive banquets I have attended where something of this sort – a sweet and sour relish – always accompanied the main meal. You may serve it in small, individual bowls, if you like. In that case, a teaspoon would be the best eating implement. It could also be served at the end of a family meal as a salad-cum-dessert.

Put the yoghurt into a bowl. Beat lightly with a fork until smooth and creamy. Add the sugar, salt, chilli powder and carrot. Mix.

Put the oil in a very small frying pan and set over medium-high heat. When very hot, put in the cumin and mustard seeds. As soon as the mustard seeds begin to pop – this just takes a few seconds – put in the sultanas. Stir once and empty the contents of the frying pan – oil and all – over the bowl of yoghurt. Mix.

YOGHURT WITH TOMATO AND CUCUMBER

Timatar aur kheeray ka raita

Serves 4–6

A cooling delight, perfect for hot, spicy meals or for eating by itself.

INGREDIENTS

450 ml (15 fl oz) natural yoghurt

About ½–¾ teaspoon salt

Freshly ground black pepper

⅛ teaspoon chilli powder

½ teaspoon ground roasted cumin seeds (p. 137)

1 smallish tomato, cut into small dice

About 10 cm (4 inch) piece cucumber, peeled and cut into small dice

Put the yoghurt into a bowl. Beat lightly with a fork until smooth. Add all the remaining ingredients and mix well.

FRESH TOMATO SALAD
Timatar ka salad

Serves 4–6

INGREDIENTS

675 g (1½ lb) tomatoes

20–25 basil or mint leaves

½ teaspoon salt

Freshly ground black pepper

⅛–¼ teaspoon chilli powder

2 tablespoons lemon juice

3 tablespoons vegetable oil (I use a mixture of 2 tablespoons peanut oil and 1 tablespoon mustard oil)

½ teaspoon cumin seeds

½ teaspoon black or yellow mustard seeds

This tastes best when tomatoes are in season. The addition of fresh basil leaves is a quirky preference of mine, mainly because they grow in such abundance in my garden and look so pretty. You could just as easily tuck in sprigs of fresh mint or green coriander.

Cut the tomatoes into 5 mm (¼ inch) slices and arrange in slightly overlapping layers on a large plate. Tuck the basil or mint leaves singly into the layers of tomatoes so that about three-quarters of each leaf is visible. Do this evenly so that the green and red are prettily distributed. Sprinkle the salt, black pepper, chilli powder and lemon juice over the tomatoes. Put the oil in a small saucepan and set over high heat. When hot, put in the cumin and mustard seeds. As soon as the mustard seeds begin to pop – this takes just a few seconds – lift the saucepan off the heat and spoon the oil and spices over the tomatoes, being careful to avoid the leaves. Serve immediately.

CARROT AND GREEN BEAN PICKLE

Gajar aur sem ka achar

Partially fills a 600–900 ml

(1–1½ pint) jar

INGREDIENTS

5 tablespoons black or yellow
mustard seeds

2 tablespoons coriander seeds

1½ teaspoons chilli powder

1 teaspoon salt

½ teaspoon ground turmeric

115 g (4 oz) green beans, trimmed
at the ends

2 medium-sized (180 g/6 oz)
carrots, trimmed and peeled

3 tablespoons lime juice

5 tablespoons corn or peanut oil

No Indian meal is complete without a proper pickle to offer its unique brand of piquancy. Of course you could buy it ready-made from an Indian grocer. But mass-produced pickles seem to suffer from a sameness of taste. This scrumptious, mustardy pickle – an invention of mine – is like no other and is quick and easy to prepare as well. It does, however, take several days to mature, but these are days when minimum effort is required: all you have to do is shake the jar a few times. It may be served with all Indian meals. You could also serve small amounts with Western foods such as roast chicken or leg of lamb, even with grilled sausages and baked hams.

Put the mustard seeds in the container of a spice grinder or clean coffee grinder and grind very coarsely for just a few seconds. Empty into a glass or stainless steel bowl. Put the coriander seeds into the same grinder and grind a little more finely – to a coarse powder. Put into the same bowl. Add the chilli powder, salt and turmeric. Mix with a stainless steel spoon.

Do not wash the green beans. Just wipe them with a lightly dampened cloth, if necessary. Cut the beans into halves, lengthways, and then in 5 cm (2 inch) segments. Cut the carrots, crossways, into 5 cm (2 inch) pieces and then into sticks the same size as the beans. Add the beans and carrots, as well as the lime juice, to the spices in the bowl. Mix well and put into a glass jar with a 900 ml (1½ pints) capacity and with a plastic lid. Place the closed jar in a sunny window for 4 days, shaking it a few times each day.

Heat the oil until it is smoking and then allow it to cool thoroughly. Pour the cooled oil over the beans and carrots. Shake well. The pickle is now ready to be eaten. It should be refrigerated and will keep indefintely.

FRESH GREEN MANGO CHUTNEY

Aam ki lonji

Makes 600 ml (1 pint)

INGREDIENTS

½ teaspoon fenugreek seeds

About 675–900 g (1½–2 lb) green, unripe mango or mangoes (see right)

4 tablespoons mustard oil (use olive oil as a substitute)

½ teaspoon cumin seeds

½ teaspoon fennel seeds

½ teaspoon black or yellow mustard seeds

¼ teaspoon kalonji

6 cm (2½ inch) piece fresh ginger, peeled and cut into fine julienne strips

¼ teaspoon ground turmeric

1–1¼ teaspoons salt

5–6 tablespoons sugar

3–4 fresh, hot green chillies

½ teaspoon chilli powder

I had forgotten about this summer delight altogether. It was not until my sister in London, Lalit, made it that I remembered how much I had loved it as a child. Memories of breakfasts and lunches with fresh pooris, vegetables and this chutney came flooding back. I realized that I had not eaten it for almost 20 years. I hope you love it as much as I do.

Now, you do need green, unripe mangoes for this. These are not just hard mangoes that are destined to be ready for the table in a few days but really unripe ones whose flesh has a greenish tinge and is quite sour. They are sold, in season – which probably lasts from April until July though produce from the southern hemisphere may make it last longer – by Indian grocers and come in all sizes, from fist-sized or even smaller to the size (but not the shape) of a hefty melon. Just ask for mangoes used to make chutneys and pickles and you will be pointed in the right direction.

For this recipe I used one very large mango that weighed about 675 g (1½ lb). It had one rather slim stone so the weight of the flesh after peeling and removing the stone was a little over 450 g (1 lb). After cutting the flesh into strips, I was able to fill a jug up to about 1 litre (32 fl oz) capacity. Because of the variation in available mango sizes, perhaps this is what you should aim for.

This recipe does require that you soak ½ teaspoon fenugreek seeds overnight. If you do not have the time to do that, just put ¼ teaspoon fenugreek seeds into the hot oil along with the cumin and other seeds.

This chutney may be served with any meal, Indian or Western. Stored in a closed jar in the refrigerator it should keep for a couple of weeks – if you do not eat it up first. My recipe is for a mild chutney. If you want it hotter, increase the chilli powder. Mangoes vary in their sourness so do taste the chutney a good 5 minutes before it is ready and then yoiu can adjust the sugar and salt, if necessary.

Soak the fenugreek seeds in 6 tablespoons water overnight.

Peel the mango and cut the flesh off the stone. Cut into strips that are 5 mm (¼ inch) thick and wide and 5–7.5 cm (2–3 inch) long. If you are in a rush, chop the flesh coarsely.

Set the oil over highish heat. When hot, put in the cumin, fennel, mustard and kalonji seeds. As soon as the mustard seeds begin to pop – this takes just a few seconds – put in the ginger. Stir and fry it for 2 minutes or until it just starts to change colour. Now put in the soaked fenugreek seeds with their soaking liquid as well as another 250 ml (8 fl oz) water and turmeric. Bring to a boil. Cover, lower the heat and simmer for 15 minutes. Add the mango, salt, sugar, green chillies and chilli powder. Stir to mix and bring to a simmer. Simmer, uncovered, on medium-low heat for 25–30 minutes or until the chutney is thick and all the mango pieces are translucent and tender. Serve at room temperature.

FRESH GREEN CHUTNEY
Hari chutney

Serves 6

INGREDIENTS

6 tablespoons natural yoghurt

2 heaped tablespoons coarsely chopped mint

2 heaped tablespoons coarsely chopped green coriander

1 tablespoon lemon juice

⅓ teaspoon salt or to taste

This chutney may be served with all Indian meals. Of course, I think it goes particularly well with the Onion Fritters on page 12 and the Indian Mashed Potatoes on page 96.

Put 2 tablespoons of the yoghurt, and the mint, green coriander, lemon juice and salt into the container of an electric blender and blend until smooth, pushing down with a rubber spatula if necessary.

Put the remaining 4 tablespoons of yoghurt into a bowl and beat lightly. Add the paste from the blender. Stir to mix.

This chutney may be stored, covered, in the refrigerator for 2–3 days.

FRESH RED CHUTNEY WITH ALMONDS

Lal chutney

Serves 8

INGREDIENTS

85 g (3 oz) red pepper (about half a de-seeded large one), coarsely chopped

20 large mint leaves or 30 smaller ones, coarsely chopped

2 tablespoons lemon juice

1 clove garlic, peeled and coarsely chopped

½ teaspoon chilli powder

½ teaspoon salt

Freshly ground black pepper

1 tablespoon blanched, chopped or slivered almonds

1 teaspoon chopped dill (optional)

This is the chutney that is traditionally served with the 'Hamburger' Kebabs on p. 24. I now like it so much I serve it with most of my meals.

Instead of fresh, hot red chillies, I have used a combination of red pepper and chilli powder. You may use the former, if you so wish. It will be much hotter. Also, walnuts may be used instead of almonds. Both would be traditional and authentic.

This chutney may be kept in the refrigerator for a few days.

Into the container of an electric blender, put the red pepper, mint, lemon juice, garlic, chilli powder, salt and black pepper in the order listed. Blend until smooth. Add the almonds and blend again. A few bits of almond may be left unpulverized. Pour into a bowl and check for seasonings. You may now mix in the dill, if you wish.

Indians generally end their meals with fresh fruit, of which we have an abundance: litchis, loquats, chikoos, jackfruit, starfruit, custard apples, strawberries, cherries, melons, mangoes, guavas, pineapples, to say nothing of oranges, tangerines, apples and dozens of different types of banana. Some people like to end their meals with a little yoghurt, natural, salted or mixed with a little sugar. Our sweets – they should be called sweetmeats – are really eaten at tea-time or at banquets.

In this chapter I have included a few yoghurt drinks and some simple halvas and fruit-based desserts. Many Indians – in a trick I am sure they learnt from the British – like to serve cut up fresh fruit, such as apples, bananas and oranges, with a simple English custard. I was brought up on this and so have included it here, though I am sure you have your own favourite custard recipe.

CONTENTS

drinks and
desserts
drinks and
desserts
drinks and
desserts
drinks and
desserts
drinks and
desserts
drinks and
desserts

BANANA HALVA

Kelay ka halva

Serves 2–4

INGREDIENTS

4 very ripe bananas

1 tablespoon vegetable oil or ghee

2 tablespoons sugar

1 tablespoon chopped unsalted, peeled pistachios

½ tablespoon chopped walnuts

4 tablespoons lightly whipped double cream or clotted cream

If you love bananas, in all forms, as I do, you will love this simple but unusual preparation. I often form the halva, which is quite malleable, into fig shapes and serve it on individual plates with whipped cream. The halva will keep, unrefrigerated, for a couple of days. Just wrap it well in cling film.

Peel the bananas and mash them.

Put the oil or ghee in a non-stick frying pan and set over highish heat. When hot, put in the mashed bananas. Stir and fry for 5–6 minutes. Turn the heat to medium and stir and fry for another 10 minutes or until the bananas have browned and turned to a kind of soft toffee. Turn the heat to low. Add the sugar. Stir for another 30 seconds or until the sugar has dissolved. Add the pistachios and walnuts and mix in. Cook to room temperature and then cover with cling film until serving time. Serve with whipped or clotted cream.

WHOLEMEAL FLOUR HALVA

Attey ka halva

Serves 4–5

INGREDIENTS

Sugar measured to the 350 ml (12 fl oz) level in a measuring jug

Seeds from 4 cardamom pods

350 ml (12 fl oz) vegetable oil or ghee

Wholemeal or chapati flour measured to the 475 ml (16 fl oz) level in a measuring jug

2–3 tablespoons mixed, chopped, blanched almonds and unsalted pistachios

This halva is generally made with chapati flour, sold by all Indian grocers, but you could easily make it with ordinary wholemeal flour. The important thing to watch for is the frying of the flour. It should turn toffee-coloured before any liquid is added or it will taste raw.

Measure everything by volume. The traditional proportion of flour:sugar:oil:water is 1:¾:¾:2 in volume. You can increase or decrease the amounts as long as you keep to these proportions. You may use ghee instead of oil for a richer halva.

Put the sugar in a medium-sized saucepan. Add 950 ml (32 fl oz) water and bring to a simmer. Throw in the seeds from the cardamom pods. Cook until the sugar has dissolved, which will take a minute or so. Set this syrup aside. Put the oil or ghee in a large, wide, preferably non-stick saucepan and set over highish heat. When hot, put in the flour. Turn the heat to medium. Stir and fry until the flour turns a warm toffee colour. This will take approximately 8 minutes. Add the syrup, stirring as you go. The syrup will make the halva bubble up. Keep stirring, turning the heat down if necessary, until the halva has thickened – a matter of a few, brief minutes. Add the nuts and mix them in. Turn off the heat and serve warm. (This halva re-heats well in a microwave oven.)

CARAMELIZED CARDAMOM APPLES WITH PISTACHIO CREAM

Sev ka murabba

Serves 4

An easy dessert that can be made with any sour, firm apples such as Granny Smiths. It may be served hot or warm.

INGREDIENTS

FOR THE CREAM:

250 ml (8 fl oz) double cream for whipping

2 tablespoons pistachios, finely chopped

FOR THE APPLES:

115 g (4 oz) unsalted butter

4 medium-sized sour, firm apples

¼ teaspoon finely ground cardamom seeds (p. 136)

⅛ teaspoon ground cinnamon

⅛ teaspoon ground cloves

140 g (5 oz) sugar

3 tablespoons blanched, slivered almonds

2 tablespoons chopped walnuts

Whip the cream lightly until it just holds shape but is not stiff at all. Fold half of the pistachio nuts into the cream. Refrigerate the cream.

Melt the butter over low heat in a large, non-stick frying pan. Take the pan off the heat. Peel, core and slice the apples thickly, dropping the slices into the butter as you cut them. Fold them into the butter as you go so that they do not discolour. (You could, if you like, keep the frying pan over very low heat as you do this.) Add the cardamom, cinnamon, cloves, sugar, almonds and walnuts. Cook on medium heat for 2–3 minutes, stirring gently as you do so. Now turn the heat to high. Cook for 8–10 minutes, stirring very gently now and then, until the apples have caramelized lightly.

Serve on individual plates with a dollop of the cream partially on and partially off the apples. Sprinkle the remaining chopped pistachios over the cream.

FRESH FRUIT WITH CUSTARD

Custard may taazay phal

Serves 4

INGREDIENTS

FOR THE CUSTARD:

475 ml (16 fl oz) milk

4 egg yolks

100 g (3½ oz) sugar

1½ teaspoons vanilla essence

FOR THE FRUIT:

2 oranges

2 bananas

When we lived with my grandfather, all 40 or so of his children and grandchildren, this was our most common dessert. Fresh fruit, mainly the apples, tangerines and bananas that we saw through much of the winter, were sliced and mixed in with cool home-made custard. I am sure it was easy to prepare then and it remains easy now.

I have used just oranges and bananas. The bananas should be sliced at the last minute.

Heat the milk in a heavy saucepan until very hot.

Beat the egg yolks with a whisk until smooth. Slowly add the sugar as you continue to beat the mixture. Stop only when it is pale yellow and thick. Now slowly pour in the very hot milk, beating as you go. Pour this egg-milk mixture back into the saucepan and set over medium-low heat, stirring all the time until it has thickened but not boiled. Boiling will curdle it. Remove from the heat and pour into a fresh, cool bowl immediately. Stir for a bit as it cools. When cool, add the vanilla essence and mix. Cover and refrigerate until needed.

Peel the oranges with a knife so that no white pith remains. Cut into 75 mm (⅓ inch) thick round slices. Now cut each slice into 6 even wedges. Peel the bananas and slice them into 75 mm (⅓ inch) rounds. Mix the custard with the fruit. Divide between 4 bowls and serve.

SWEET, PALE ORANGE, MANGO LASSI

Aam ki lassi

Serves 2–3

INGREDIENTS

300 ml (10 fl oz) natural yoghurt

250 ml (8 fl oz) chopped, ripe mango flesh

3 tablespoons sugar or to taste

¼ teaspoon ground cardamom seeds (p. 136)

8 ice cubes

Soothing and satisfying, this could be made with the peeled flesh of fresh ripe mangoes or with good tinned ones. Drain the tinned mangoes before using them.

Combine all the ingredients in an electric blender and blend. Some ice pieces may remain. Pour into 2–3 glasses and serve.

PALE GREEN SPICY, MINTY LASSI

Hari lassi

Serves 2

I cannot think of anything more refreshing for a hot summer day.

INGREDIENTS

300 ml (10 fl oz) natural yoghurt

3 tablespoons chopped green coriander

25 large mint leaves or 30 smaller ones

1 cm (½ inch) piece fresh ginger, peeled and chopped

½ fresh, hot green chilli (use the upper half for more heat, the lower for less), coarsely chopped

⅓ teaspoon salt or to taste

¼ teaspoon ground roasted cumin seeds, optional (p. 137)

8 ice cubes

Combine all the ingredients in an electric blender and blend until smooth. Some ice pieces may remain. Pour into 2 glasses and serve.

Utensils

While no extra-special utensils are needed for preparing Indian meals, it does help to have the following:

WOK OR KARHAI

A karhai is just an Indian wok. It tends to be a bit more rounded but performs the same function as the wok. Both are half-moon shaped and both are excellent for deep-frying and stir-frying. It is also useful to get slightly rounded spatulas that best fit the wok's shape.

ELECTRIC BLENDER OR FOOD PROCESSOR OR BOTH

In India, a grinding-stone is used for grinding garlic, onions and ginger. Electric machines are less romantic but also less wearing on the body. They work fast. One very useful way of finely chopping onions, garlic or ginger involves throwing them into a food processor and then starting and stopping the machine with great rapidity until the desired result is achieved. This is known as the 'pulse' method.

COFFEE GRINDER

Dry spices cannot be ground in blenders or food processors. Only a clean coffee grinder will do. I keep an extra one for the purpose. Just wipe off with a dry or very lightly dampened cloth when you are finished with it.

PRESSURE-COOKER

A pressure-cooker is necessary only for speed. Meats such as beef, lamb and pork will not stew fast any other way. Out of all the pressure-cookers I tested, the one I liked the best – it really made cooking a breeze – was a Kuhn Rikon, made in Switzerland. It comes in many shapes and sizes. I have the one that resembles a frying pan. The bottom of these pans, even though they are all stainless steel, is virtually non-stick and the opening and closing mechanisms work as if they had been freshly oiled. There is no separate weight that has to be placed on the top and no frightening, hissing noises as the cooking proceeds. A truly wonderful gadget.

NON-STICK PANS

I like non-stick pans. They make my cooking easier. The heavier the pan, the better its quality usually is. Pans with the same brand name may come in different weights. Look for the one that is the heaviest. Nowadays, one can find pans where the non-stick element is so well bonded to the bottom metal that the two are inseperable. These are ideal. Use wooden or plastic spatulas and spoons when cooking with these pans so that you do not scratch the non-stick surface.

TONGS

Tongs come in very handy when you need to turn pieces of meat over or pick up grilled or fried chicken pieces or when you need to delve into a sauce to remove, say, a bay leaf. Make sure the tongs move easily before you buy them. Stiff tongs are virtually useless.

GINGER-GRATER

A ginger-grater looks like an ordinary grater but has no holes or openings. It can only be found in stores that sell oriental cooking utensils and is generally made in Japan. Some Japanese grocers sell it. I find that I just cannot do without my ginger-grater. It grates ginger to a pulp in seconds and, what is best, holds the rough fibres back while allowing me to collect the pulp.

Techniques

HOW TO PEEL AND CLEAN PRAWNS

Most prawns available in the West already have their heads removed. If this has not happened, first pull the head off. Now, pull off the dangling feet. Peel the shell, which should come away in rings. Pull away the shell on the tail. Make a shallow cut along the back of the prawn and remove the vein. Put all the cleaned prawns in a bowl. Rub with 1-2 tablespoons coarse or Kosher salt. Wash the prawns. Rub with salt one more time and then wash well and drain. Pat the prawns dry and store in a well-closed polythene bag in the refrigerator until you are ready to cook.

HOW TO PREPARE AND CLEAN SQUID

Twist off the head (with the tentacles). Cut off the hard area near the eyes but retain the head. Squeeze or pull out all the soft stuff still left inside the tubular body as well as the hard cartilage-like 'pen'. Peel the fine skin on the tubular body. Now wash both the body and the head with salt as suggested for the prawns. Drain and pat dry. Store as suggested for the prawns.

MAKING YOGHURT SALADS

Always beat yoghurt lightly with a whisk or fork until it is smooth and creamy before adding cucumbers, onions or any other solid ingredients. This is particularly true of home-made yoghurt. It stays lumpy if this is not done.

DEEP-FRYING

Make sure that the oil is hot enough before you add the ingredients to be fried. If a medium-low or medium temperature is called for, set the heat to that temperature. Wait 5–7 minutes for the oil to heat up. Then put in a small piece of bread. If it begins to sizzle immediately, your oil is ready for deep-frying.

TARKA OR THE TECHNIQUE OF FRYING WHOLE SPICES IN HOT OIL

In China, cut spring onions are dropped into a little hot oil and the combination is dribbled over a freshly steamed fish. In parts of the Mediterranean region, similar effects are achieved with olive oil and garlic. In India, we would call this technique tarka or baghaar. We might use quite a few spices and seasonings to achieve a more complex result. Dishes in India can be given both a final flavouring or an initial flavouring by heating oil and then, when it is very hot, putting in whole spices such as cumin seeds or mustard seeds. The spices are allowed to sizzle and pop for a few seconds. Foods such as small boiled potatoes or raw cauliflower pieces are then added to the pan to be stir-fried or else the contents of the pan – oil and spices – are poured over, say, a dish of cooked legumes.

An Indian store-cupboard

AJWAIN SEEDS

These small seeds look rather like celery seeds and are sold only by Indian grocers. In this cookery book, I have replaced them with dried thyme as the aromas are somewhat similar. If you manage to get ajwain, use only half the quantity as it is quite strong.

ASAFETIDA

A brownish resin of strong odour, asafetida is used to give a special kick to Indian foods. Even though used in small quantities, it subtly tranforms the taste of a dish. It also happens to be a digestive. For easy use, buy the ground variety.

BASMATI RICE

Now quite easily available, Basmati rice is long grained and quite aromatic. For best texture, it should be washed before being used even though many packagers suggest otherwise.

CARDAMOM

A highly aromatic spice, cardamom is generally sold in its pod form. Indians like to use the green pods but most supermarkets seem to stock the bleached, less aromatic whitish pods. Use whatever you can get. If cardamom seeds are called for, either remove them from their pods or buy them loose from an Indian grocer. To grind small amounts of cardamom seeds, use a mortar and pestle. When cardamom pods are used whole, they should not be eaten.

CHAPATI FLOUR

This is a very finely ground wholewheat flour sold only by Indian grocers. The best substitute for chapati flour is a mixture of wheatmeal and plain flour in equal proportions.

CHICKPEA FLOUR

Also known as gram flour and besan in Indian shops and *farine de pois chiches* in French and other speciality shops. Chickpea flour is made from grinding dried chickpeas. I store mine in the refrigerator to discourage bugs.

CHICKPEAS

Because dried chickpeas take a long time to soak and cook, I have used only tinned ones in this book. Drain the chickpeas well and then rinse them out before using them. This gets rid of their tinny taste.

CHILLIES

These tend to be slim and about 5–10 cm (2–4 inches) long. They are generally green, but when they ripen they can turn red. The hottest part is at the stem end where there are a lot of seeds. Chillies tend to vary in their heat. Always wash your hands carefully after cutting them.

Dried red ones are the same chillies, ripened and dried. I generally use them whole to lessen their heat but take advantage of their flavour.

CHILLI POWDER

This is the ground version of the dried red chillies.

COCONUT MILK

For the purposes of this quick and easy book, use only good-quality tinned coconut milk. It should be creamy white and not oily. A brand I like is Chaokoh, a product of Thailand. This is sold in Indian and South-East Asian stores. Unless sugested otherwise, stir the tin well before use as the cream tends to rise to the top.

CORIANDER, FRESH GREEN

A very popular herb in India. To store coriander, put it, roots first, into a tall glass of water. Cover with a polythene bag and keep in the refrigerator. When a few tablespoons are called for pull off a handful of leaves and tender stems from the top, wash and pat dry, and then chop as the recipe requires.

CORIANDER SEEDS, WHOLE AND GROUND

Whole coriander seeds are beige and round and the ground version is one of India's most common and cheapest spices. Buy small quantities of ground coriander only as it will lose its flavour within a couple of months.

CUMIN SEEDS, WHOLE AND GROUND

Shaped rather like caraway seeds, cumin seeds, in their whole and ground forms, are used with great frequency in Indian cooking. Both forms are sold by supermarkets and Indian grocers. To make ground roasted cumin seeds, put 4–5 tablespoons of the whole seeds into a small cast-iron frying pan set over medium heat. Stir the seeds and roast over dry heat until they turn a few shades darker and emit a wonderful roasted aroma. Wait for them to cool slightly and then grind them in a clean coffee grinder. Store in a tightly closed jar. This is a useful spice to have on hand. It will last a good month or two though its flavour will gradually lessen.

Black cumin seeds are finer than regular cumin seeds and much more expensive. I use them to make my own garam masala.

CURRY LEAVES

These highly aromatic leaves should only be used in their fresh form. Many Indian grocers sell them. Curry leaves are shaped like bay leaves but are much smaller. Many leaves are attached to a single stem and can be removed easily with one fluid movement of the fingers along the stalk. They can be stored in the refrigerator in a polythene bag. They can also be stored in the freezer the same way. Do this while they are still fresh and green. They may then go straight from freezer to pan.

GARAM MASALA

My own recipe for this spice mixture requires 1 tablespoon cardamom seeds, a 5 cm (2 inch) cinnamon stick, a third of a nutmeg and 1 teaspoon each of black peppercorns, black cumin seeds and cloves, all thrown into a clean coffee grinder and ground to a powder. However, to make matters easier, I have mostly suggested the use of store-bought garam masala. All Indian grocers sell it. When a recipe calls for the store-bought version, do not use my recipe, even if you have some on hand. The tastes are quite different.

GHEE

This is butter that has been clarified so thoroughly that you can even deep-fry in it. As no milk solids are left in it, it does not need refrigeration. It has a nutty, buttery taste. All Indian grocers sell it.

GINGER, FRESH

Ginger is a knobbly, brown-skinned rhizome. It should be peeled before being used. When I refer to a 2.5 cm (1 inch) or 5 cm (2 inch) piece of ginger, just take that much off the length of the rhizome. Do not worry about the width. When very fine slivers are required, cut the peeled ginger, crossways, into very fine slices. Then, stacking a few slices together, cut lengthways into very fine strips. When 'ginger grated to a pulp' is required, peel the ginger partially but leave the peeled knob attached to the main rhizome. Using the main rhizome as a handle, grate the peeled ginger on the finest part of the grater to get a soft pulp. The Japanese sell special graters for ginger. Get one if you can find one.

KALONJI

Small tear-shaped black seeds sold by Indian grocers.

CURRY POWDER

In the interests of speed, I have turned to a rather good brand of curry powder, Bolsts. I like their hot curry powder. You may use any brand you like.

FENNEL SEEDS

Shaped like cumin seeds but plumper and greener, fennel seeds have an anise-like flavour.

FENUGREEK SEEDS

Yellowish and squarish, fenugreek seeds give curry powder its special odour.

MUSTARD

The Pommery mustard I have used in this book is a substitute for mustard seeds ground in vinegar. It is a coarse, grainy French mustard that is also labelled *Moutarde de Meaux*. Dijon mustard is generally smooth and is easily available.

MUSTARD OIL

This is a wonderful oil. Get to know it. The best substitute for mustard oil is a fruity olive oil. The flavours are quite different but the richness is similar.

MUSTARD SEEDS, BLACK

These are sometimes black, sometimes reddish-brown. The yellow mustard seeds sold by most supermarkets may be used as a substitute. To grind mustard seeds, just put them into a clean coffee grinder and grind very briefly.

PEPPER CORNS

It is best to buy black pepper in bulk. Major Indian grocers sell it in 450 g (1 lb) and 2.25 kg (5 lb) bags. Store it in closed cannisters in a dark, cool place. Buying it from supermarkets in small jars seems so much more expensive.

RED LENTILS

Known as masoor dal in Indian shops. I have used red lentils in this book as they cook quite fast.

TURMERIC

The dried, very yellow powder from a rhizome. Turmeric can stain so be careful when using it.

VEGETABLE OIL

I like to use groundnut or corn oil for most of my cooking but you may use another simple vegetable oil if you prefer it.

YOGHURT

Indians use only natural yoghurt in their cooking, which is made or bought as unseasoned and unsweetened. Buy any natural yoghurt that you like. I find that the rich, creamy yoghurts as well as those made from skimmed milk are generally quite satisfactory for any of my recipes that require it.

Suppliers

BRISTOL SWEET MART

80 St Marks Road

Bristol BS5 6JH

Tel: 0117 951 2257

Fax: 0117 952 5456

Website: www.sweetmart.co.uk

(Ethnic foods and spices; mail order)

FIFTH SENSE TRADING COMPANY LTD

Trinity House

Lisburn BT28 2YY

Northern Ireland

Tel: 028 9260 6870

Fax: 028 9260 6879

Website: www.FifthSense.com

E-mail: orderInquiries@FifthSense.com

(Ethnic foods and spices; mail order)

CURRYBOX.COM

21 Devonshire Avenue

Allestree

Derby

Derbyshire DE22 2AU

Tel: 01332 553572

Website: www.currybox.com

E-mail: orders@currybox.com

(Spice boxes; mail order)

THE SPICE SHOP

1 Blenheim Crescent

London W11

Tel: 020 7221 4448

www.thespiceshop.co.uk

(Spice blends, cooking accessories; mail order)

WORLD FOODS

181 Penarth Road

Grangetown

Cardiff CF11 6JW

Tel: 029 2039 4618

Website: www.world-foods.co.uk

(Rice, spices, pickles, pastes, oils, flour; mail order)

Index